The

Campaign

Manager

**Running & Winning
Local Elections**

**By
Catherine M. Golden**

Published by
Oak Street Press
886 Oak Street
Ashland, OR 97520

Library of Congress Cataloging-in-Publication Data 96-92023

Golden, Catherine M.
      The Campaign Manager: Running and Winning Local Elections/by
      Catherine M. Golden

Includes index.
ISBN 0-9650761-0-5
1. Local elections--United States--handbooks, manuals, etc.
2. Campaigning management--United States--handbook, manuals, etc.
3. Electioneering--United States--handbooks, manuals, etc.
4. Political Science and Government

Editors: Michael E. Holstein, Ph.D. and Matthew Farmer, J.D.

Brochures and ads by Brian Freeman, Crystal Graphics

Cover and Book Design by Catherine Greene, Greene Communications
      Medford, OR

Back Cover Photography by Christopher Briscoe, Ashland, OR

Computer consultant: Bryan K. Devendorf

First Edition: 1st Printing 1996, 2nd Printing 1996, 3rd Printing 1997

Manufactured in the United States of America

Dedicated to my children, Daniel and Sarah,
who have shared me, nearly all their lives,
with the community I love.

❧

A special thanks to all the volunteers
who make running for and serving
in public office so rewarding.

Contents

Preface

Running for local office can be one of the most demanding and exhilarating experiences of your life. Your house will be cluttered and chaotic, your children ignored, and your partner, whether involved or not, will be stressed. And yet, seeking office or pushing through a ballot measure gives you an opportunity to be a leader, effect change in your community, and repay something to the city, county, state, or country that you love. You will also find the campaign experience offers an opportunity for you to grow personally. You will be challenged and stretched as you never have been before. When all is over, win or lose, you will be a different person, with a different outlook on our political process and a new respect for those who run and serve.

Since 1985 I have worked on or run many campaigns in my region. When I first started campaign organization, I was overwhelmed and could find no written information to give me comfort or guidance. Through years of experimentation and collaboration with other seasoned campaigners, I found organizational techniques that worked in political campaigns, and I began to apply them to the campaign process. The more success I had on campaigns, the more I was asked to help with or speak to campaign committees to get them started. I spoke to groups at campaign schools and was continually asked to provide simple "how-to" information for campaign teams. This book is the culmination of campaign trial and error. It gives you the tools needed to organize the efforts of others on your behalf. Whether you are a novice or seasoned campaigner, you will find information here that will make your efforts more organized and effective.

Good luck and have fun.

"You have to be smart enough to understand the game and dumb enough to think it's important."
Gene McCarthy on how politics is like coaching football

How To Use This Handbook

In this section

The Framework
The Layout
Know the Law

Running a local election can seem a bewildering, complicated process. It involves recruiting volunteers, raising money to run the campaign, analyzing how best to allocate people and money, projecting the best image and message, and getting out the vote.

This handbook breaks a campaign down into manageable units for easy implementation. If you are the candidate, you will find the necessary tools to run your own campaign. If you have either a paid or volunteer campaign manager, this handbook will organize and guide the two of you and your team through the campaign process.

Because of the complexity of the campaign process, take time to read this entire handbook, especially before you design your campaign flow-chart. A campaign makes more sense as a whole.

The Framework

In local politics, there are generally three types of political campaigns:

- Partisan: Democrat vs. Republican vs. Independent

- Nonpartisan: two or more candidates, with no party affiliation, square off. These elections usually have no primary, only a general election.

". . . the seeds of political success are sown far in advance of any election day. . . . It is the sum total of the little things that happen which leads to eventual victory at the polls."

J. Howard McGrath, Former Chairman, Democratic National Committee

• Ballot measure or proposition: these represent single issues brought to the voter by a governing body. An initiative or referendum is a single issue brought to voters by a citizen group. Neither involves candidates.

A partisan race differs from other campaigns only in how the precinct analysis is performed for the primary. For example, if you are involved in a partisan race in the primary, that is, two Republicans running against each other, you will look at the voting trends of Republicans only, just as you will if you are a Democrat running against another Democrat. In all nonpartisan or ballot measure races, you look for past voting trends on that issue, regardless of party affiliation.

A campaign measure differs mainly in how it starts. If it is being referred by the voters' initiative or referendum, it will begin with signature gathering. However, if a government body places the measure on the ballot for you, then this campaign is run exactly like any other.

The "formula campaign" that is the basis for this book is a way of systematically organizing other people's efforts on your behalf. You provide the guidance in setting up volunteer systems for phoning, clerical support, fund raising, lawn sign dispersal, and canvassing. Within each of these, critical organizational work is necessary to accomplish a variety of tasks. These tasks include such things as putting together your campaign team and volunteer organization, developing a campaign theme and message, designing campaign brochures and lawn sign art, performing precinct analysis, designing direct mail, handling the media, presenting the candidate, following a flow-chart, and overseeing campaign clean-up.

After reading this handbook, determine what your campaign is capable of, then use this handbook to provide the blueprints for completing those tasks successfully. By breaking a campaign down into manageable units and organizing the activities within each component, you will never overload your work-force. Once you have decided what you can or want to do in organizing your campaign, you will need to plot these activities on a campaign flow-chart. Many campaigns use a "campaign plan" as a way to track the necessary upcoming campaign activities. Instead, I prefer a more visual "campaign flow-chart" because it presents a campaign time line at a glance.

The Layout

Following this brief introduction, Chapter 1, "The Campaign Team," covers the small select group that will develop campaign strategies and lend the support and expertise needed to win. Chapter 2, "The Campaign Brochure," details the single most important thing the campaign team will do in the campaign: develop a campaign theme and message. It is also the first task of the team.

Chapter 3, "Volunteer Organization," gives you the basis for organizing your phone banks and clerical workers. Chapter 4, "Fund-raising," helps you raise money in a variety of ways using your volunteer force. In Chapter 5, "Lawn Signs," I discuss the design, placement and maintenance of signs. Chapter 6, "Precinct Analysis," gives you a step-by-step methodology for directing campaign resources where they will do you the most good. If your campaign has an especially busy schedule, precinct analysis is actually something that can be done months ahead of the campaign kick-off. However, I have placed precinct analysis in Chapter 6 because it must happen prior to canvassing and getting-out-the-vote, which are outlined in Chapters 7 and 8.

Chapters 9 and 10, "Direct Mail" and "Media," cover what has become the most expensive aspects of a campaign. Along with all the necessary information to make the most out of direct mail and media, you will also find tips in each of these chapters to stretch your campaign dollars. Chapter 11, "The Candidate," is about projecting a positive image before the voters and thereby minimizing the potential nit-picking that the public might do. And Chapter 12, "The Campaign Flow-chart," puts in chronological order all that you will need to do to win. Although laying out a flow-chart is one of the first things you will do to organize your campaign, without a baseline knowledge of the first 10 chapters, it would make no sense.

Finally, Chapter 13, "After the Ball," is simply about winning and losing gracefully, putting your campaign to bed, and election night. For ease in applying this handbook to a campaign, I have included all forms mentioned in the text under the "Appendix."

Know the Law

Visit the county clerk and or city recorder to become familiar with state and local election laws. For example, in my city, you are not allowed to place lawn signs more than 30 days prior to an election. You also are not allowed to place them on the median strip between the sidewalk and street. Although, the homeowner may plant, mow, and care for this area, it is, in fact, public property. To place a lawn sign here could be interpreted in one of two ways: either you feel you're above the law or you don't know it. Either interpretation is a problem if you hope to be in government.

"Play for more than you can afford to lose and you will learn the game."
Winston Churchill

It is against federal law to place campaign literature in and around mailboxes. The federal government owns your mailbox, even though you bought and installed it, and it can be used only for the U.S. mail. Also note that, because publicly-owned buildings are maintained, lit, and owned by the taxpayers, they may not be used for campaign purposes.

The county clerk or city recorder will also draw attention to filing dates that you and your treasurer must know. Missing a campaign expenditure filing deadline will almost always get you media coverage, just not the kind you need or want. Other than the legal materials that you will want to get from the county clerk, city recorder, or the secretary of state, everything you need to run a successful campaign is included in this handbook.

Chapter 1

The Campaign Team

In this chapter

The Campaign Committee
The Treasurer
The Campaign Manager
The Campaign Chair or Co-Chairs
Finding Volunteers
Potential Volunteer Sources
Volunteer Sign-up Sheet

For the purposes of this handbook, the campaign team refers to those who help organize your efforts. It is the committee, the treasurer, your volunteers, and each of the individual teams that oversee a portion of the campaign. Your media team, for example, may have a liaison to the campaign committee, but it should be looked upon as part of your overall campaign team. Aspects of the campaign team will be covered in this chapter. However, campaign efforts which involve large numbers of people and independent efforts, such as lawn signs, media, brochure development, and fund-raising, will be covered in separate chapters.

The Campaign Committee

The campaign committee serves two functions: first, it is a support group, both for itself as well as the for the candidate or measure, and second, it is the primary source of expertise for the campaign. This small, select group will maneuver and steer a campaign while drawing on the resources of the

"Campaign teams are important for one single reason: A collection of heads is better than one."
Sharon Schaefer

community. The committee should consist of individuals who have different personal strengths and areas of ability.

Your campaign committee is a real insiders' group. The candidate and each of the members must feel safe to speak candidly without worry. Treat them like insiders, and keep them informed of any campaign development. Welcome their criticisms. You would never want a committee member to first learn about a problem with the campaign in the newspaper. Call your committee members often. Encourage them and support their individual efforts in the campaign. Listen carefully to determine if they might need additional help. Be clear about their tasks, expectations, and time commitment.

Take time in choosing the right number of people for a campaign committee. I have worked on county-wide campaigns with four committee members (including the candidate), which was too few, and city-wide campaigns with twelve members, which was too many. I have found that six committee members for a city up to 20,000 is perfect. In county-wide campaigns a successful committee also might include members from each city who oversee teams within their respective cities.

You want only enough committee members to cover the campaign activities that you have decided to do. Keep in mind that not all campaign activities occur at the same time, so it is often possible to have more than one task assigned to a single committee member. For example, the campaign brochure is written and printed at the front of the campaign, whereas the demands on the canvassing coordinator are greatest at the end of the campaign. On the other hand, fund-raising responsibilities and clerical worker coordination are both on-going and should *not* be the responsibility of one person.

Once the campaign starts, I meet with my committee each week for one hour. For city-wide campaigns where people are not traveling great distances, I like to do this in the evening after 8:00 or 8:30 PM because children are hopefully in bed and the day's work is done. Up to a point, the later you meet the better. Why? Because people are ready for their day to be done, so they arrive on time and get right down to work. Few people function well after 10:00 PM, so at 9:30 you're ready to call it quits. Never let a meeting go beyond one hour unless it is the first meeting and you're setting up the campaign. If this is the case, allow additional time by starting the meeting earlier, or move the first meeting to a different time—for example, a morning retreat followed by lunch where the campaign becomes official. For county-wide campaigns, it works well for the committee to meet in a central location at the end of the work day before dinner.

"Someone needs to be the gas, someone the brakes, and someone needs to steer this thing."
Mary Greenwood

Your committee may quickly break down into specialized campaign functions. Once specialized groups are formed, keep track of their progress by getting reports back each week. When the committee meets, I want the meetings to be productive and for people to feel it is time well spent. I always have an agenda on an easel and often have a task for the committee members to do while we are covering the agenda (for instance, brochures can be folded or envelopes stuffed). It is important that all meetings begin and end on time.

Besides the weekly meeting for the full committee, it is necessary to get together occasionally with individuals responsible for specific campaign tasks. Sometimes, for example, I will meet with my ad person to hammer out two or three ads. I will then bring these to the regular committee meeting to have them critiqued.

Other than the treasurer, the makeup of your committee is optional, and you must decide how many people will be needed to plan and supervise the campaign. You will depend on the people you invite to join your campaign committee, so they should be capable of organizing and directing some particular aspect of the campaign. Your committee, in addition to a treasurer, may include a campaign manager and one or more people to oversee letters-to-the-editor, canvassing, clerical work, brochures, the media, lawn signs, phone banks, fund raising, and your volunteer workers.

The Treasurer

Campaign treasurer is almost always a volunteer position. Selecting the right person is one of the most important things you will do. The name of your treasurer will appear on every campaign publication. He or she will be called from time to time by the press, or even the opposition, and asked questions. Like a vice-president in a presidential election, the treasurer should balance the ticket. For example, if you are a retired senior, get a prominent, involved, young person of the opposite sex. If you are a young progressive man and relatively new to your community, consider an older conservative woman who has been in town a number of years. Find a person who complements rather than merely repeats your strengths. If you're a Democrat, find a respected Republican. Ideally, if you are working for more taxes for schools, get someone who is conservative and who may have spoken at some time against tax increases.

If possible, find someone willing not only to represent the campaign and discharge the official duties of treasurer, but to perform other tasks as well. For instance, I try to get someone who will not only handle all the treasurer's responsibilities but will oversee the thank-you notes for contributions as well.

The treasurer is usually responsible for obtaining and completing the registration forms required for participation in an election. The necessary forms can be obtained from the city recorder's office for city races, from the county clerk's office for county races, and from the secretary of state for state legislative races. Don't be afraid to use these offices. The people who staff government offices are often extremely helpful and accommodating.

Not all the forms and information in the election packet are necessary or applicable to every race or election. Ask for help from the clerk's or recorder's office on exactly what you need to read, what is required, and when it is required. Ask either the clerk or recorder to direct you to the pertinent dates for filing your campaign contributions and expenditures. While the filing of these reports is the principle job of the treasurer, it is a good idea for the candidate and campaign manager also to be aware of them. These can be placed on your campaign flow-chart as a reminder.

Contributions and Expenditures

Your treasurer should be a stickler for detail. The opposition will be examining your contributions and expenditures (C&E) filings for any mistake to report to the state elections office. If one is found, it is bound to make the paper. That sort of thing is unbelievably damaging to a campaign and is totally preventable.

Following the filing of the C&E forms, local papers generally do a story on who spent how much on what. If you are running a modest campaign and your opposition is funded by outside money, make sure your committee points that out to the media. Running a visibly hard-working campaign with modest funds gives people the sense that you are fiscally responsible. That trait is desirable in office, and people will make the connection.

While it is difficult to work on a campaign where the opposition has unlimited funds, it can also work in your favor. In a small community election with no TV involved, there is just so much ad space to buy in the newspaper, just so much direct mail that can be sent to homes without it becoming pretty clear that the election is being bought. In one campaign I ran, we were outspent nearly five to one by the opposition, and we publicized this spending discrepancy to our advantage. When the newspapers ran the usual C&E article, many in the community were stunned by the amount of money coming in from outside interests. Since we had a pretty good idea of how much they were spending, we were ready when the press called for our reaction. Supporters wrote and sent letters-to-the-editor for those who missed the newspaper articles when they first appeared.

"In life, as in any game whose outcome depends on both skill and luck, the rational response to bad odds is to try harder."
Marvin Harris

The opposition was convinced that our accounting was wrong and sent people to the recorder's office on a regular basis to check our C&Es. This is where having a meticulous treasurer paid off. Finally, convinced of foul play, the opposition called the paper and suggested there must be something amiss. When the press called me, I explained that we were in fact spending a normal amount of money for a small-town race, and it was the opposition whose money numbers were excessive. We got another great newspaper story.

Committee to Support

Given the importance of a good treasurer, what do you do if you can't find the right one for you? Not to worry. You have two options. First, you can place a short list (six to nine) of carefully selected supporters at the bottom of all your literature and ads. This "Committee to Support" should represent a good cross-section of the community. Although some of these people might be working on your campaign, this is not your work crew. The primary job of this group is to give your cause credibility by lending their names. Depending on the issue, the committee may include people in business, environmental groups, real estate, labor, and so on.

Using a "Committee-to-Support" works well if you have broad support up front, but not at all if your support is marginal. I once worked on a campaign that was so controversial that I could get only three names to sign the committee-to-support list. Rather than have such a short list, which didn't cover the political spectrum of the city, I dropped the notion of listing the committee. In fact, finding out about the level of controversy was good information to have early in the campaign. It made us work that much harder.

Another option you have if the "right" treasurer cannot be found is to simply press on. Continue to look for someone who is thorough, honest, easy to work with, trustworthy, and committed to your cause or candidate. Ask friends and associates to suggest people who work with numbers to support you. Talk to your personal accountant or the person who prepares your taxes. CPAs have good community credibility, and they may be willing to provide report preparation pro-bono.

The Campaign Manager

Of all the tasks in a campaign, asking someone to be the campaign manager is the most difficult. Where other jobs have finite responsibilities and time commitments, the job of campaign manager is open-ended. It is a lot to ask of anyone, especially on a volunteer basis. For this reason it is usually the first and sometimes the only position to be paid.

"Loyalty is more important than experience."
Bill Meulemans

A campaign manager will interact with your volunteers more than any other person in the campaign, so good communication skills are a must, especially phone skills. The duties of the campaign manager vary greatly depending on the number of individuals working in the inner circle. In general, he or she will do such things as attend coffees, debates, and events with the candidate and set up sign-in sheets while lending moral support. The campaign manager also *must* give candid feedback to the candidate without being too blunt.

If you are running a county-wide partisan election campaign, a manager is critical. You will need someone to oversee it all and to be a source of support for the candidate. If your campaign is to pass a local ballot measure, you can serve as the campaign manager with the use of this handbook. If you are running for office in a small city, you probably don't need a manager. However, without one you will need capable people to head up various campaign tasks such as lawn signs, canvassing, and letters-to-the-editor. The most effective campaign teams I have employed have been volunteer teams I supervised myself.

Potential Sources for Campaign Manager

I highly recommend teachers as campaign managers. They are smart, organized, articulate, and personable. They are able to speak to large groups of people and ask for things in simple, understandable ways. They tend to know computers, have a nice collection of presentable clothes, work hard, and are generally politically savvy. They are also likely to be available all summer. If you do it correctly, a teacher who is a campaign manager will force you to get everything ready during the summer so that your fall campaign goes much easier. The drawback of using a teacher is that he or she may be overwhelmed with school responsibilities in the fall and not be available to the campaign.

Other potential sources for campaign managers or workers are fund-raisers or development directors for local charities, private schools, or non-profit organizations. These people might consider short-term work for a candidate, and they will have a proven track record. Other leads: people who have worked on other political campaigns, for a United Way campaign or for a Heart/Lung Association fund-drive; those who have organized local parades, 4-H fair shows, music concerts, or county fairs; or individuals who have served as development chairs on local boards.

I have always structured my own election campaigns so that my manager and I run the campaign together. This setup makes it a lot easier to ask someone to take on this huge responsibility. In general, a good campaign manager is hard-working, organized, intelligent, self-confident, and loyal.

And, because appearance is important, this person should reflect the values of the candidate or campaign.

Maintaining Control

Recently, I was a campaign advisor where the campaign manager became problematic. He was parking illegally on city-owned land and then hassling the police with a "do-you-know-who-I'm-working-for" attitude. To make matters worse, volunteers were complaining to the candidate about the campaign manager who was being unnecessarily rude. The candidate was at the end of his rope and called me to help find a way to let this volunteer go.

While a candidate does not need this kind of stress in a campaign, firing a volunteer who wants to work on a campaign can bring more headaches than it cures. So short of firing the manager, what can the candidate do?

First, the candidate always has the option of reorganizing the campaign so that the manager has less involvement and responsibility. Second, the candidate could deal with the campaign manager and the situation in a clear and straightforward manner. He or she could kindly explain how the manager's actions were being interpreted by others and how they were reflecting negatively on the campaign and the candidate. Because campaign managers are so closely affiliated with the candidate, there is an assumption that their activities are both known and endorsed by the candidate. A problematic situation like this must get immediate attention. While campaigns are a way for the community to see how a candidate will perform both publicly and under pressure, it is also a time for the candidate to get some experience in dealing with awkward situations and people. Once in office, they materialize all the time.

The Campaign Chair or Co-Chairs

When working on a ballot measure it is helpful to have a visible leader heading up the campaign. A campaign chair or co-chairs can serve this purpose. This person or couple may serve in name only or as the campaign co-coordinators. Most times, other than the speakers' bureau, these people become the face of the campaign. They meet the media, they meet with the campaign committee on a weekly basis, and they work the endorsement circles of the community: the Rotary Club, Chamber of Commerce, business leaders, and more. They gain power and stature when they seemingly have nothing to personally gain by the passage of the measure. So avoid, for example, using a county commissioner for a county tax base.

Choose your co-chairs carefully. They should be people who are well-respected within the community, and they should have established relationships with other prominent local leaders. You will depend upon these existing relationships to help establish your ballot measure, raise money, and activate volunteers.

Well selected, hard-working chairs can win a difficult campaign for you. I like to have co-chairs and prefer they be a man and a woman. If it is a county measure, I will look for one who is respected and involved in the urban community and for another who is involved in the unincorporated area. Selection of your chair or co-chairs is completely dependent on the ballot measure. For example, if the measure is for school taxation that augments revenues for extracurricular activities, then bring in two individuals who have different interests and involvement in the schools. One might be a big supporter of sports and the other foreign language. A nice touch here might be someone who has been outspoken in the past against school funding measures coupled with someone who has been very involved in supporting school programs.

I have worked on ballot measures with co-chairs and no chairs. Each way has its strengths and weaknesses. If you cannot get what you feel would be the "right" chair or co-chairs, don't use any, but be sure you have top people to respond to the press and willing to debate the opposition.

Finding Volunteers

Finding and directing volunteers is almost the same for each campaign task. Although the tasks vary considerably, only a small modification is necessary to organize your volunteer force for each specialized campaign activity.

Regardless of the activity, as with the campaign committee, there are seven important things to remember about using volunteers:

1. Don't waste the volunteers' time. Have everything laid out and ready to go the moment they walk in the door. Begin and end on time. Do not reward late arrivals by delaying the start of the meeting.

2. Be prepared with anything they might need. If the task is to stuff envelopes, make sure there are enough stamps, sponges, pens, staples, and other necessities.

3. Call them ahead of time and let them know what they need to bring, for example, extra staplers, clip boards, good walking shoes, a truck.

4.   Be clear about their tasks, expectations, and time commitments. Give clear written instructions and deadlines.

5.   Pick the right people for the job. Don't ask out-of-shape people to canvass hillsides; don't ask counterculture people to canvass conservative areas.

6.   Keep them informed; support them. When you call, let them know how the campaign is going. Be sensitive to their schedules.

7.   Treat your volunteers as though they are highly paid employees.

There is a tendency to value volunteer time less because it is free. This is a serious mistake. When you are disorganized and waste your volunteers' time, they are bound to feel frustration and irritation. If it happens more than once, they will not be back. Even if it happens only once, you could lose your best people and have trouble getting the support you need. To avoid such problems, assemble a clerical team to help set up other tasks. For example, a clerical team could staple lawn signs in preparation for the lawn sign team who will be putting them up or have clerical people look up phone numbers before phone bankers arrive. This is actually more important than you might realize; different types of people agree to different types of jobs — looking up numbers and phoning are very different tasks. This pre-planning is vital to volunteer success.

Matching Volunteers to Skills

Although a small campaign can be run without volunteers, it would be a mistake to do so. When people work for you, they have an investment that they want to see pay off. It is also a terrific part of the political system because it gets people interested and involved in government. There is one caution, however. If workers tell you they do not want to do a particular activity or that they are not good at something, believe them.

I once placed a woman on the phones who told me she didn't like to phone. I found it hard to believe that anyone would have trouble talking on the phone, also I was desperate for callers. What a mistake. She was painfully uncomfortable calling people she didn't know and projected a poor image of the campaign. I couldn't take her off once I saw my error. That would have called further attention to the problem, making her more uncomfortable. I left her on the phone for about a half hour and then told her that I had finished my work and asked if she would mind if we shared her phone. She gratefully gave it up. Similarly, if someone says he or she hates to canvass, believe it. It is better for the campaign to have people doing tasks they enjoy.

I try to supervise my volunteers to make sure I do not bring back poor workers a second time. For instance, if while I am supervising a phone bank I see people struggling, I simply note it on their 3x5 volunteer worker cards and pull the color circle that indicates "phone volunteer" (see Chapter 3, "Volunteer Organization: Methodology"). That way I will not call those persons again to work the phones, and everyone will be much happier. Similarly, if I discover workers who are great at a task like phoning, I try to keep them away from other campaign activities to avoid burning them out. Hopefully, I can use them again in tasks where they excel.

The same kind of supervision is necessary for each volunteer activity. For example, if a canvasser returns without notes for lawn signs, no impressions of voter attitudes, and a partially-covered area, I know I have a volunteer who isn't particularly good at knocking. I remove the canvassing color code from his or her 3x5 card, make a note as to why, and move that person over to something like lawn sign placement and maintenance. You never want your volunteers to have a bad time if you can avoid it. You want to keep people working for you in election after election.

Potential Volunteer Sources

If you're involved in politics, you have to be able to find people who, for whatever reason, are willing to help you. Finding volunteers can be a lot of work. Remember, however, that the only people you can be absolutely certain will not help you are those you do not ask. The following is a list of places to look:
- *Your family, friends, and business associates*
- *Women's rights groups*
- *Former candidates, office holders, and their volunteers*
- *Local service groups*
- *Labor unions*
- *Teachers or school associations*
- *Any special interest groups dealing, for example, with the environment, human services, hunting, fishing*

In nearly every election there is an issue so controversial that people will decide to vote for you based on your position alone. These voters are called "ticket splitters," and the result is that sometimes rather than working *for* your candidate, these people are motivated by issues that make them work *against* the opposition.

"We make a living by what we get. We make a life by what we give."
Winston Churchill

In general, ticket splitters translate into both volunteers and money for your campaign. Here is a list of some groups and issues that are more inclined than most to let a single issue influence their votes:

- *Veterans*
- *Sportsmen, fly fisherman, hunters*
- *River guides*
- *Environmentalists*
- *Timber, logging advocates*
- *Clean air advocates*
- *Pro-choice, anti-choice supporters*
- *Fire fighters*
- *Bicyclists*
- *Land use advocates*
- *Seniors*
- *Tax and anti-tax groups*
- *Gay rights activists*
- *Identifiable work groups such as teachers*

Volunteer Sign-up Sheet

In addition to finding volunteers in the groups listed previously, you can use the form on the next page for sign-ups at coffees and debates once the campaign is under way. (A full-sized form for photocopying is included in the "Forms" section at the end of this book.) The information gathered on the sign-up sheets is then transferred to the 3x5 volunteer card described in the next chapter.

VOLUNTEER SIGN-UP SHEET

I would like to volunteer for the following (please check all that apply):

Name (please print)	Home Phone	Canvass Neighborhoods	Phone Banks	Lawn Sign Location	Donation

Fig. 1.1 Example of Volunteer Sign-Up Sheet.

Chapter 2

The Campaign Brochure

In this chapter
Polling

Brochure Development

Pictures

Campaign Slogans

Logo

Layout

Sample Brochures

Before you sit down to write a brochure, you must first develop a campaign theme and message. To do that, your campaign team must assess the strengths and weaknesses of your candidate or ballot measure. Ask and answer, who will vote for your candidate or ballot measure over your opposition and why. You must also look for the fatal flaws of your candidate or measure. The campaign message and theme will develop from this process and will become the foundation for your slogan, ads, and media responses. Once you have a message, do not get off it, and don't let your opponents pull you off.

In this process you will identify issues that will create a relationship between your campaign and the voters. For example, your candidate has worked hard for clean air issues. That knowledge helps you establish a relationship between the County Clean Air Coalition and your candidate.

"Leaders can conceive and articulate goals that lift people out of their petty preoccupations and carry them above the conflicts that tear a society apart."
John W. Gardner

Another example: people in a particular neighborhood are concerned about development; your campaign issue includes a park in close proximity to their homes. You use this information to create a relationship. This concept is important in direct mail, ads, brochure development, speaking engagements, debates, and campaign endorsements, and will get further attention in those sections and chapters. Get these relationships established early, and, when the time comes, they will help with absentee ballots and early money.

Very simply, you want a majority to see your side as right and the other side as wrong. This is the time to assess the strengths and weakness of your opponent, if you have one, or the opposition, if your campaign is about an issue. The brochure is basic to your campaign. You will walk it door to door, mail it to households, or hand it out at debates. People who receive it must get the message of your campaign, which will state in subtle and not so subtle ways why people should vote for your campaign cause. Obviously you will be giving your brochure to people inclined to vote for you or your measure, and the message of the campaign will reflect that voter propensity.

Polling

Conducting a poll may be the most efficient and accurate way to determine voter concerns prior to developing your message. While it is important to have elected officials who lead their constituency from a set of core values, as Rosalynn Carter said, "It is difficult to lead people where they do not want to go." Having a clear reading of voter concerns will help your campaign develop and direct a message where it will be best heard.

Because polls must be either professionally conducted or supervised, they tend to be expensive. To cut costs there are a couple of things you might consider. First, offer to include other candidates if their campaigns will contribute to the cost. And second, some firms will come down in price if you provide the workers for the poll. Be aware that, depending on the length of your poll, this may be an enormous undertaking. However, because it can be done long before your kick off, it is often possible to do a poll without adding too much extra stress.

Besides getting you information on voter concerns, polls can also tell you:
- *How age groups break down: what age supports your candidate, your measure, your opponent*
- *The education of those supporting you or your opposition*
- *The gender of your support*
- *Your name recognition, the recognition of your opponent, and whether that recognition is favorable or not*
- *The length of time those being polled have lived in your community*

"Leaders are people who step forward, who influence thinking and action. They emerge to meet the needs."
    William Gore

- *Whom the voter will support if the campaign were held tomorrow*
- *What the voter does for a living*
- *Party affiliation*
- *If they intend to vote*
- *Issues of interest in the community*

If a labor union, teacher's union, or a PAC supports you, ask if their organization would be willing to conduct a poll on your behalf.

Brochure Development

While the campaign committee will help to develop the campaign message and theme, I usually have only one or two people work with me or the candidate in writing the brochure. Obviously you want a good writer who has a couple of free days. The writing takes only a few hours followed by many rewrites. These rewrites will often go before the committee to check message and theme, and before I go to the printer, my committee always reviews the final draft.

If you write your own campaign brochure, you must have someone read it critically when you finish writing it. The emphasis here is on *critically*. We all love our own words, and our friends are often loath to condemn them. You need someone you can trust, who has political savvy to read your work, correct errors, and make suggestions.

Pictures

Prior to sitting down and laying out a brochure, I visit a photographer. I have always been fortunate to work with local professionals willing to contribute to my campaigns with their talents. I have tried using friends with above-average equipment, but nothing compares to professional work. Amateurish photos hurt your campaign. If a professional will not volunteer his or her time, this is a good place to spend money. If the first sitting does not produce the "right" photo, be willing to invest in a second shoot.

When you are campaigning for ballot measures, photos are much easier to come by. For example, if you are working on a school tax base, visit the yearbook class at the high school. They save photographs of all age groups, in all activities. If you need photos for a park program, try the YMCA. For historic photos of your city or county, try a local historian. Most photographers will let you use their photos if they can have bylines.

I use pictures as a way to break up the text and give the brochure a feel. Most brochures for candidates contain at least a picture of the candidate. This is important to increase recognition. With that recognition comes familiarity

"Keep it simple."
Jeff Golden

that is important psychologically for the voter. The candidate begins to feel like a friend and a celebrity all at once. You may also carefully select other photos to create an image of who this person is. There may be pictures of the candidate at work, with the family, at play (e.g., softball game or fly fishing), with seniors, at a preschool, a public school, a hospital, or a park. Include whatever might both positively connect the candidate with his or her lifestyle and also characterize what is important in the community. Be sure the photos are not all taken in the same clothing.

If the brochure is about a measure, such as a school levy, show what will be accomplished with the passage of this measure through pictures as well as text.

Depending on your budget and the size of your brochure, you may just stop with the picture of the candidate. But if you have more, be sure the pictures add to or underscore the story you have selected for the text. Put thought into your selection of pictures. Try to show the diversity of your community in the photos: people of all ages and color, working class and professionals, men and women.

Campaign Slogans

Years ago, slogans were printed next to a candidate's name on the ballot. At that time, with media playing a lesser role in politics, having a catchy slogan was critical for a win on election day. Slogans can still be very effective. However, to be effective, slogans require a great deal of thought by the campaign committee. Do not invent a slogan just to have one. Know your campaign message and design a slogan that furthers that theme. Sit with your committee, list the strengths of your candidate or measure, and brainstorm on a slogan. Then once you think you have one, brainstorm on all the ways it could be used against you or hurt your cause. Work at this process until you come up with the right combination.

The slogan should be a simple statement about why you should be elected or why the voters should vote for your measure. Your slogan must not depart from your campaign message and should evoke a gut emotion. One very effective slogan used in an environmental race simply said, "Share the Water." Who can argue with the idea of sharing? It is a friendly thought and is encouraged throughout our lives. It also implies that the water is not being shared presently or may not be in the future.

I was on a campaign that used the slogan "Now Let's Choose Leadership." I was concerned that this slogan would sound patronizing. I was further concerned that those who had voted for the incumbent in previous elections would feel we were belittling them for past votes. It was especially

"Leaders have a significant role in creating the state of mind that is society."
John W. Gardner

problematic given that many misinterpreted our candidate's quiet nature as aloof and arrogant. This slogan tended to reinforce that perception.

For a local restaurant tax to fund a sewer treatment plant, our opposition used the slogan "Don't Swallow the Meals Tax." I thought this was a really clever slogan and still do. It works because it hits us on so many levels. People who swallow something are duped, and then of course it was about food.

In one open-space campaign, we used the slogan "Parks, Now and Forever." People who opposed the measure saw ours and used the slogan "Parks: **Pay** Now and Forever." A very clever counterslogan. We should have chosen ours more carefully.

During my first run for mayor, I used the slogan "Building a Better Community." I chose this because of city-wide concerns regarding growth and development. I wanted a positive slogan that suggested to people the subtle message that more was not necessarily better and that it was a community that needed to be built. In my second run I did not have a slogan because I was reusing some of my old lawn-sign stock and because my new signs were busy with graphics. The second sign did not need to say anything because the picture was the message.

The following are examples I have pulled from brochures in my files, some good, some bad. Using a slogan is optional. Better to omit it than have a bad one.

> *"The best . . . for the best"*
> *"For Change, For Choice, For Us"*
> *"A voice that will be heard"*
> *"We all win with [name]"*
> *"A leader for [name of the place]"*
> *"A concerned candidate for all of [place]"*
> *"Leadership in Action: [name]"*
> *"A Strong Voice for [place]"*
> *"With his experience . . . It makes sense"*
> *"Vote for the Future . . . vote for [name]"*
> *"[Name] is in touch . . ."*
> *"Because nothing counts like results"*
> *"Straightforward, Fair, Effective"*
> *"Tough, committed, fighting for us"*

There is always an abundance of campaign slogans that underscore experience. It is my opinion that voters place very little value on political experience, unless you are running for a specialized position, such as county clerk or city recorder.

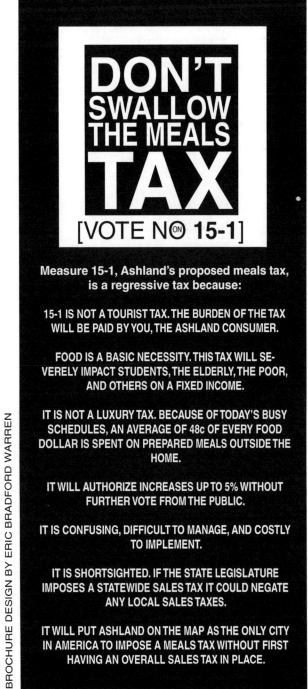

BROCHURE DESIGN BY ERIC BRADFORD WARREN

DON'T SWALLOW THE MEALS TAX

[VOTE NO ON 15-1]

Measure 15-1, Ashland's proposed meals tax, is a regressive tax because:

15-1 IS NOT A TOURIST TAX. THE BURDEN OF THE TAX WILL BE PAID BY YOU, THE ASHLAND CONSUMER.

FOOD IS A BASIC NECESSITY. THIS TAX WILL SEVERELY IMPACT STUDENTS, THE ELDERLY, THE POOR, AND OTHERS ON A FIXED INCOME.

IT IS NOT A LUXURY TAX. BECAUSE OF TODAY'S BUSY SCHEDULES, AN AVERAGE OF 48c OF EVERY FOOD DOLLAR IS SPENT ON PREPARED MEALS OUTSIDE THE HOME.

IT WILL AUTHORIZE INCREASES UP TO 5% WITHOUT FURTHER VOTE FROM THE PUBLIC.

IT IS CONFUSING, DIFFICULT TO MANAGE, AND COSTLY TO IMPLEMENT.

IT IS SHORTSIGHTED. IF THE STATE LEGISLATURE IMPOSES A STATEWIDE SALES TAX IT COULD NEGATE ANY LOCAL SALES TAXES.

IT WILL PUT ASHLAND ON THE MAP AS THE ONLY CITY IN AMERICA TO IMPOSE A MEALS TAX WITHOUT FIRST HAVING AN OVERALL SALES TAX IN PLACE.

ADD a 5% TAX TO YOUR CHECK

[Ashland Meaure 15-1]

Back   **Front**

Fig. 2.1 Brochure layout, two-panel, front and back. Note that the front and top back of the brochure are visually striking, but the lower, dense, reverse type is hard to read.

Logo

I regularly use the lawn sign logo on my brochures. I think it adds continuity to a campaign, giving a subtle message that it is well organized and well thought out.

Layout

The layout of a brochure depends on how it is to be printed. Unless you know the business, you will need the help of a layout artist or graphic designer.

A good way to get ideas on layout is to go over past political campaign brochures. Often you can find the look you want and then copy that look. Some examples of different types of brochures can be found following this section, but your best resource will be the politically experienced graphic designer or layout artist.

Although many experienced campaigners believe brochure copy should be kept to a minimum, I worry about offending the astute voter with an empty brochure. I usually have quite a bit of information in my brochures and assume if people do not want to read it, they don't have to. However, the text should be broken up with pictures and graphics. Unappealing brochures will be read by no one, even the most sophisticated voter. There are a number of ways to get your messages out, for example, a letter from the candidate, testimonials, or pictures, and it is best to bullet information items. Brochures are advertisements, so they must catch the eye. Once you have caught the attention of voters, they might appreciate a little more information.

Brochures on a tight budget can be done easily. A brochure may be laid out three up on a single piece of paper. This way each piece will yield three brochures (see example *Fig. 2.2*). With the cost of paper this is an incredible savings. Although each sheet of paper must be cut in thirds, cutting costs are less than the folding costs of the previous example. Pictures add very little to the cost, and the visual relief is quite effective. Use them. I have even used card stock for this type of brochure. By using card stock, you have the advantage of being able to shove the brochure into door jambs.

Obviously, the size of your brochure is determined by the size paper you use. Go to a print shop and check out colors and sizes. In a few campaigns on which I've worked, we used legal-sized paper folded in half. This size lends itself well to easy layout and visual impact.

As the size increases, the layout gets more difficult, the paper price increases, and the brochure becomes more expensive. Decide both how much you need to say and how much you can afford to say. When the content and layout of the campaign brochure are mocked up, be sure to run it by your campaign committee for final approval.

Sample Brochures

Fig. 2.2 Brochure layout, three up. This is the front of a single-panelled canvassing piece with candidate information on the back side. This way, each piece of paper will yield three brochures.

Fig. 2.3 Example of brochure layout, three panel. The inside might include a map of the proposed area or text and pictures. With this particular design, the essential information is on the front panel. For those who look further, more in-depth information can be included throughout. If you choose, the front two questions can be changed for little additional printing cost. This way, your campaign can deliver specialized brochures to targeted precincts.

YES ON 53 & 54

Parks

now and forever

On May 15, 1990, we'll be voting on a proposal to preserve 730 acres of parkland for the future. The plan reflects months of suggestions expressed in many public hearings and neighborhood meetings by a variety of concerned citizens.

1. WHY SHOULD WE CARE?

Ashland's special beauty lies in its setting, its use of open space and its pedestrian lifestyle. To preserve this beauty for our children, we must set aside area for parks and open space now.

2. HOW MUCH WILL IT COST ME?

Beyond extremely small indirect costs, the plan will cost each household $6 per year in the form of a .50 per month surcharge on utility bills.

Paid for by the People for Parks Committee, Fred Binnewies, Treasurer, PO Box 1, Ashland, OR 97520

Chapter 3

The Volunteer Organization

In this chapter

Methodology

Applying the Methodology

Phone Banks

Phone Bank Locations

Clerical Workers

No matter where you find your volunteers, you still have to organize them and direct their efforts toward activities that will win you the election. Keeping track of your volunteers and assigning them responsibilities requires some sort of organized system. Although the following system can be adapted to a computer, the process I have set up here does not require one.

The methodology that is outlined in each of these activities really works. If you use it as outlined, you will almost never have no-shows. More to the point, you will be able to utilize your volunteers better and thus run a more effective campaign. Running an effective campaign means you have done all you can do to run the campaign as efficiently as possible. If you do that, win or lose, you, your committee, and your volunteers can feel very good about what you have all accomplished.

"Politics is 3x5 cards."
Bill Meulemans

Methodology

Here is how to keep track of campaign volunteers:

Make a 3x5 card for everyone contacted by the campaign. Make a card even if it turns out that the person contacted does not support your candidate or cause. Do this because there had to be a reason the person was contacted in the first place. After hundreds of calls, you'll forget and waste time by calling again. Keep the 3x5 cards you fill out for each person contacted together in one box, regardless of what that person says he or she is willing to do. Each 3x5 contact card is set up exactly the same.

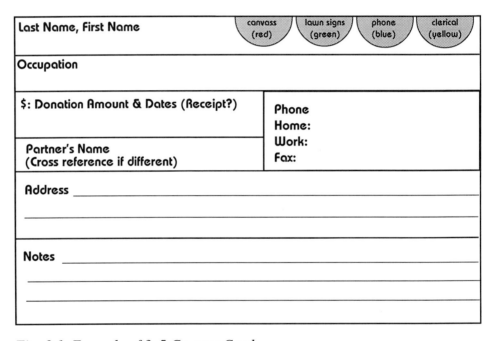

Fig. 3.1 Example of 3x5 Contact Card

It is important to keep track of donations since some states have filing requirements for anyone giving more than a certain amount of money. In addition to the information recorded on the card, fold over colored circle stickers, working from the upper right hand corner toward the left. Place the sticker so that it looks like a half-circle on each side. If you do this, you can see the coding from the top of your index card box. You may also just color in half circles with marking pens, but this means that you will have to generate a new card if it turns out people can't do an activity they are coded for.

The color coding indicates which campaign activities, such as lawn signs, phone, canvass, or clerical work, the volunteer will work on. Feel free to alter the color scheme to fit your campaign. Be aware, however, that using more than four color codes can be a bit much on a 3x5 card. For my campaigns, I use a green circle for lawn-sign help; blue for phones; red for canvass; and yellow for clerical. The color coding is a quick way to access who can do what. Because the colors are visible from the top of your index box, the cards can be easily pulled or flipped through to get names and phone numbers. This way you do not have to read each and every card to see what an individual is willing to do for the campaign. You will also be less inclined to sort according to activity, thus misplacing or scrambling cards. There will be cards with no color coding. The coding indicates *workers*, but remember, nearly *everyone* you contact will make it into this box.

The "Notes" section on each card is important and helpful. This is where you can remind yourself what volunteers have told you. If, for example, you have someone who is coded to canvass but cannot do it until October, that information gets noted on the card. Special needs or skills relevant to assigned activities get noted here as well (e.g., "won't canvass hills," "Don't call early AM," "Don't call after 8:00 PM," "Horrible on phones"). I also use the Notes section if someone has been rude. I do not want to call them back (or have a volunteer call them), and your team needs to know why. After hundreds of phone calls you will not remember who said what if you don't have an accessible written record. Whatever the comments, the color coding remains the same.

Organize Volunteer Activities

Once information is on the 3x5 cards, you're ready to set up volunteer activities. The following process works for activities such as phone banks, clerical work, money, canvass, and lawn sign placement or maintenance. To organize a campaign activity, use 5x8 lined index cards set up as shown on following page.

Once you have the 5x8 cards prepared, proceed as follows:

1. Pull the names and phone numbers from the appropriate 3x5 index cards and transfer this information onto the 5x8. (The 3x5 cards should never get far from their box.)

2. Whatever the activity, have a number of dates lined up so you have to call your potential volunteer only once. If you are calling for an ongoing activity such as canvassing, have four or five dates and times. If one date doesn't work, another will. If none work, that

gets indicated on your 3x5. However, the name you have called should remain on your 5x8 with a line through it. In this way, you will remember that you called and that they could not do it. If you do not do this, believe me, you will forget and call again.

3.   A couple of days before the activity, every volunteer gets called back. That is what the "CB" column is for. My preference is to talk to my worker, so I leave messages only as a last resort. I never call to ask my workers if they are still going to canvass. Of course they are; they told me they would. I don't even call to remind them of the canvass. If they are very organized, they will resent the call. I call and remind my canvassers to bring a clipboard or ask if they mind doing hills or check to make sure that I gave them the correct meeting place or the correct time. Whatever it is, it's my fault or my screw-up, and I'm just checking to make sure I gave the information correctly. If they have forgotten, this reminds them. If they accidentally made other plans, here is my opportunity to reschedule. Potential no-shows, discovered by a phone call, are incredibly easy to reschedule.

Activity: Canvass 10/14				
NAME	PHONE #	CB?	9:30 am-12:00	2:30-5:00 PM

Fig. 3.2   Example of 5x8 Canvass Activity Card

Applying The Methodology

Every campaign consists of basic campaign activities, such as:
- *Running phone banks*
- *Canvassing the voters*
- *Developing a campaign brochure*
- *Designing ads, media*
- *Organizing clerical support (including thank-you notes)*
- *Getting up lawn signs*
- *Raising money*

Each of the these activities is volunteer intensive. You can apply the general techniques developed above to find and keep track of volunteers. However, each activity requires specific techniques. The above methodology will be applied throughout this handbook to organize each of the activities.

Phone Banks

Phone banks can be used throughout a campaign and are the most efficient way to retrieve information in a short period of time. They can be used to get a head-count for a fund-raiser, to get lawn-sign locations, to raise money, and to get the campaign more volunteers. If you plan to do a get-out-the-vote-effort on election day, you will have to identify (ID) voters who intend to vote for your candidate or cause. This can be done while canvassing, but it is easier and far more efficient to do it by phone.

When you are ready to organize a phone session, use the following procedure:

The 5x8 Card Set-Up

1. Go to the 3x5 box and pull the names and numbers of phone bankers. It can be helpful if a friend calls from a separate list, such as The League of Women Voters, but check the lists you are calling so people are not called twice. Make sure someone will follow through on calling from home.

2. List the potential volunteer on your 5x8 card below the headings, as shown on the following page. If you have more than one date and time available, you will have better luck placing the volunteer with a single call.

3. As you call people, sign them up for a particular date or time. If they cannot work, cross them out so you can still see their names. This way you will not forget and call again. Lastly, remember to

"Luck is the crossroads where preparation and opportunity meet."
Anonymous

call them back one or two days prior to the phone bank. Check your CB column when you do.

Activity: PHONE BANK						
[IF YOU HAVE MORE THAN ONE DATE, YOU CAN ADJUST AS FOLLOWS]						
NAME	PHONE #	CB?	(FIRST DATE)		(SECOND DATE)	
			1st Hour	2nd Hour	1st Hour	2nd Hour

Fig. 3.3 Example of Phone Bank Activity Card

4.   Assure people that they will be trained to work on the phone before actually doing so.

5.   Never assign a phone banker to work more than one hour and 15 minutes (15 minutes for training and then one hour on the phone.) Almost anyone will give up an hour or so for a campaign they believe in, and if it turns out that the volunteer is bad on the phone, an hour is plenty.

6.   Have two to three shifts each night. Individuals must arrive 15 minutes before their shift for training. No one likes to go on the phone cold, so people rarely miss training when it's offered and expected.

7.   After a 15-minute training session, volunteers begin to call. The first 20 to 30 minutes that volunteers are on the phone, I circulate and answer questions. I do not get on the phone myself, especially in this first 20 minutes of a shift.

8.   The next shift arrives 15 minutes early for training or 45 minutes into the hour of the previous shift. This way, exactly one hour after the first shift starts, they get a tap on the shoulder from someone on the next shift, and they are off the phones.

9.   Never tell people that you want them for a specific amount of time then push them to stay longer. You will lose them as volunteers. When you ask someone to work for you, you have made a verbal contract with them for a specific job and a specific amount of time. Don't nudge.

10.   Do a role play with your volunteers—have one volunteer pretend to call another.

11.   Do not expect your phone bank people to look up phone numbers. Use a clerical team of volunteers to do that ahead of time.

12.   Always have prepared scripts in case a phoner needs one; however, the caller who ad libs will do best.

Phone Bank Training

The following is an example of what you might prepare for your volunteers who are phoning for the campaign:

Before You Pick Up The Phone—

1. *Be proud of what you are doing.* You are working for a cause you believe in. You are on the front line of a campaign.

2. *Think about what has motivated you to give up your time to work for the candidate or ballot measure.* People will ask how a candidate stands on a particular issue. While you cannot speak directly to that, you can share why *you* are working for this individual (or cause).

3. *Identify yourself as a volunteer working for the campaign.* In general, you want only one name to make it into the consciousness of the voter, unless, of course, you know the person.

4. *No matter what else happens, get <u>something</u> from the individual before you get off the phone.* "You can't canvass, ever? How about a lawn sign?" "You have a bad lawn-sign location? Do you have a friend who might want one?" "Can we use your name on the endorsement ad?" "Would you make a contribution?" Whatever. You want them in on the campaign with that single call, or to know how they will be voting. (This is helpful information for the campaign.)

Fig. 3.4 Example of Phone Bank instructions

What you ask for will vary according to the phone bank. For example, you could be calling for lawn-sign locations, money, volunteer workers, a head count for an event, Voter ID (that is, simply the process of finding out if a voter supports your campaign or not). Think about your mission, and prepare a short introduction for the caller. Sample scripts follow in this section.

Phone Bank Locations

It can be difficult locating enough phones to run an effective phone session. I have found that realtor offices work best because they usually have five or more lines in the same room. People love to have company when calling. I have also used law offices, although this is a little more touchy due to confidentiality concerns and the fact that callers can't see each other. Sometimes, campaign headquarters for a bigger race (such as president or governor) will let you use an office. You might also try labor union or insurance offices. Many businesses will support a cause or a candidate and open their doors for phone banks after hours if you simply ask.

Make no assumptions: On one campaign, a realtor who was working for the opposition let us use his phones because we were friends.

Scripts

Wherever your phone bank is located, the important part of campaign phoning is to have an effective message. You should have scripts made up in advance for each campaign activity. While it is preferable to have people ad lib, they generally need a prepared script for the first couple of calls. It gets much easier after that. Do not have volunteers give their names as it just adds one more bit of clutter in the introduction. I also don't have anyone ask, "How, are you doing tonight?" The reality is the volunteer doesn't care, and the person on the other end knows it. So just cut to the chase. Here are some possible scripts for typical campaign phone sessions:

Lawn-Sign Location
    "Hello, I'm a volunteer working for the 'Cathy Golden for Mayor' campaign. We're looking for lawn-sign locations tonight. Will you be supporting Cathy in the general election? Great, could we place a lawn sign? Let me verify your address. Someone will be coming by a month before the election to place it. We also have a crew who will be maintaining these signs; however, if it needs some attention, maybe you could help with it. Great. Thanks." Hang up.

Special Activity

"Hello, I'm a volunteer working for the 'Cathy Golden for Mayor' campaign. Did you receive the invitation for the campaign dinner this Saturday? We are trying to get an idea of the number of supporters who will be attending the dinner for Cathy. The restaurant needs a pretty accurate head count. Will you be joining us?"

Canvassing

"Hello, I'm a volunteer working for the 'Cathy Golden for Mayor' campaign. We're doing a last minute, get-out-the-vote door hanger. We are hoping to canvass the city in two hours and need about 85 volunteers to hang brochures on people's doors. There will be no door-knocking, just great exercise. Can you help?"

Another. . .

"Hello, I'm a volunteer working for the 'Cathy Golden for Mayor' campaign. Our notes indicate that you might be willing to canvass for the campaign. Is that correct?" (Answer) "Great. I have a number of dates for some upcoming canvasses. Do you have your calendar handy?"

I'm assuming that most people are as busy as I am, and I try to get the message out in pretty short order. These give you the general idea.

Undecided

On any of these scripts, if I call and discover that someone is undecided or leaning, I ask whether the individual would like more information from the candidate or campaign committee to help him or her decide. Finally, whatever a potential supporter might say, I ask my volunteers to make a note so that the campaign can follow up if need be.

Negative response

Make a note for the campaign and get off the phone as quickly as possible.

Clerical Workers

The clerical team is an extremely important part of your campaign. Normally you think of people sitting around, stuffing envelopes, stamping, and labeling. While these tasks might comprise the bulk of your clerical team's efforts, you should think of this function in broader terms.

Wherever I can break activities down into more manageable units, I do so. For example, on the day that lawn signs go up, you *cannot* expect your lawn sign team to arrive early in the morning, staple lawn signs, organize lists, and then head out for two hours of stake pounding. In reality each of those functions is very different and should be treated differently.

Your clerical team can come in days ahead of time to staple lawn signs or attach them to the stakes, depending on the type of sign you use. They can come in on still another day to help organize the lists, maps, and locations of where those signs are going.

Your clerical team is crucial in keeping your campaign tight and organized. Use them creatively wherever they can help with your work-load or with the organization of an upcoming activity. Here are some examples of how the clerical team can be used:

* *Staple lawn signs at the corners (if using poly tag).*
* *Attach lawn signs to stakes (if using corrugated).*
* *Look up phone numbers for an upcoming phone bank.*
* *Assemble maps for a canvass.*
* *Attach inserts in the brochures for a canvass.*
* *Write thank-you notes for money, lawn-sign locations, or to volunteers.*
* *Stuff, stamp, and address a mailing.*

To set up a campaign activity requiring clerical workers, proceed as follows:

1. Across the top of lined 5x8 cards list the words: "Name," "Phone #," "CB," and the dates for your clerical work party. (Time is much *less* flexible here than in most volunteer activities.) I usually have clerical parties that last two hours. List your clerical workers under the "Name" column that you have retrieved from your 3x5 cards, as explained earlier in this chapter.

2. If you need help getting volunteers, try senior groups that support you, The League of Women Voters, and your friends and neighbors. Given how much fun a clerical party can be, it is usually pretty easy to turn out a crowd.

3. The clerical work party is a social time in campaigns for me, a time to chat with friends that I sometimes see at length only during a campaign. We share war stories about a canvass or whatever while having coffee and cookies and doing a mindless task. These meetings are enjoyable and highly productive for the small amount of effort involved.

Activity: Clerical Work Party				
[IF YOU HAVE MORE THAN ONE DATE, YOU CAN ADJUST THIS AS FOLLOWS]				
NAME	PHONE #	CB?	(First Date & Time)	(Second & Time)

Fig. 3.5 Example of Clerical Work Party Activity Card

It is important for people to be comfortable while working and sitting for two or more hours, so be sure to do it where there is enough table space for each volunteer. Do not do clerical work in an already cluttered house. I also hate working on a soft, over stuffed couch or chair. Because of the age of my clerical work party and the general disintegration of our backs (young and old), I take the time to put together a comfortable work area.

4. I always have some snacks around—coffee, tea, cookies, and the like—but not on the table where work is being conducted.

5. Have everything set up. Do not waste your volunteers' time.

6. Do one activity at a time: if it is getting out a mailing or stapling lawn signs, do just that. When the task is done, usually ahead of schedule, don't bring out one more thing for people to do. Remember, as I said before, with this task, as with any other in a campaign, you have made a verbal contract with your workers. Once they are captive in your home, to ask for more work past the designated time or task creates hard feelings. Workers who complete a task early and go home feel good about their participation and feel that they are helping in a well-organized effort.

7.   Make sure that you have all the necessary materials at each station so people are not idle. Have extras of everything you need, staplers, sponges, stamps, envelopes, telephone books, rubber bands, or whatever else the task might require.

Chapter 4

Fund-raising

In this chapter

Campaign Budget

Direct Mail for Money

Special Events

Holding a Special Event

Candidate Calls to Raise Money

Calling for Money for Ballot Measures

Your campaign theme and message are critical to a successful fund-raising effort. As indicated previously, the message is developed early so you can attract support from special interest groups promptly. This message and the relationships that develop result in endorsements and money. The endorsements will come from individuals, companies, political action committees, and formal organizations who feel your cause will further their efforts. Early endorsements = early money = early media buys.

In every campaign I have worked on, individual contributions tend to arrive at the end of the campaign. Supporters see the campaign in the paper and on television and hear it on the radio. They know that this takes money. What they do not know is that media time must be bought weeks and sometimes months in advance of when it will air or go into print. Early money is critical to a successful campaign. That is why many people take out personal loans to get the campaign rolling.

Know the law: in some states you may not legally begin collecting money until you have filed with the county clerk or city recorder.

Campaign Budget

Although this handbook has no formal budget sheet, it is a good idea to make a cursory one. List activities you intend to perform and make a few phone calls for cost estimates. If you plan to do TV or radio ads, individual stations will have people in sales to help, but bring along someone with experience in this area.

A pretty reliable ballpark figure as to the amount of money you will need to raise is $1.00/household in the voting district. If you have strong opposition, you will need more ($3.00/household); if you have weak opposition, you'll need less. I am not talking voters in a district; I am talking households. The type and amount of media buys will greatly influence this figure, because it is just about the only thing that can't be donated.

Everything you do in a political campaign requires money. While many of the people who work for you will also give you money, the bulk of it will come from those not directly involved as volunteers.

I never apologize or feel like I am begging when I ask for money for a candidate or measure. I assume that the potential contributor wants this person in office (or the benefits of the measure) and is willing to back up that support with money to get the election won. When I ask for money, I think of it as asking for less than asking for a person's time. How many times has someone called you to volunteer your time, and you thought how much you would prefer to give money instead? The reality is this: if you can find excellent candidates to volunteer their time to be in office implementing programs that you support, more power to them. Do all you can to help get them there.

In the State of Oregon, anyone who contributes to a political campaign may file for a state income tax *refund* of up to $50. If a husband and wife file a joint tax return, they can get a refund of $100. Sadly, only about 16% of citizens take advantage of the refund. The refund tends to level the playing field for grassroots campaigns. If your state has a similar program, find out about it and get this information to your potential donors.

Direct Mail for Money

While direct mail can help create a relationship between your campaign and the voter, it is also an opportunity to raise money where those relationships are established. Given that efficient direct mailing requires a mailing list of some already identifiable group of voters, I prefer to see which lists I can get and then formulate a letter or piece that will appeal to those

"Apart from the ballot box, philanthropy presents the one opportunity the individual has to express his meaningful choice over the direction in which our society will progress."
George Kirstein

voters. However, remember, *your direct mail is only as good as the list to which it is sent.* Carefully match your appeal to people you are targeting.

In a direct mail piece, you might include a targeted letter, a campaign brochure, and a remittance envelope. Direct mail can be used to simply align your candidate with an issue such as a concern for jobs where unemployment is high, parks and playgrounds where there are none, or anti-growth in a neighborhood where a big development is targeted. If you include remittance envelopes with your direct mail pieces, be sure to color-code them so you know who is responding to what. That way you get some feedback on which letters were most effective, along with the money. I color code my envelopes by running a marking pen along the edges of a stack of envelopes.

Special Events

Special events are campaign-sponsored activities intended to raise money and support for the campaign, for example, a coffee at a supporter's house or a campaign-organized luncheon, dinner, or picnic. Although I have done many special events for campaigns, compared to the candidate calling supporters directly, they raise very little money and take untold amounts of campaign time. The people who attend are usually supporters who have already given and have every intention of voting for your candidate or cause.

With all of that said, it is important to stress that fund-raisers are not only about raising money. Special events are also for public visibility and education, for involving volunteers so they are more committed to the campaign and candidate, and for promoting "friend-raising" by strengthening bonds volunteers and guests have with the candidate. I have had great success with a few events.

Thus, when approached as an opportunity to advertise the candidate and cement relationships, special events can be worth the commitment of resources necessary. But don't underestimate the commitment involved. You need to be cautious about the strain special events put on the campaign committee, volunteers, and the candidate. If someone other than the campaign committee is sponsoring the event, as is often the case with a coffee, you need to be ready to help that event be a success.

Ensure a Good Turnout

The one thing you must avoid if you schedule a special event is a poor turnout. If it looks like a fund-raising event will have marginal attendance, I invite all my volunteers to attend for free. Not only can I thank them with a free meal, but numbers are more important than money when holding a special

"We are so busy doing the urgent that we don't have time for the important."

Confucius

event in political circles. Whatever the attendance, you need to be certain that the people who do attend don't have a bad experience. If for some reason people can't find the location, or can't find parking or feel uncomfortable in the situation, they are likely to blame you.

A common special event problem is someone's name being accidentally omitted from a guest list. You can turn this potentially very embarrassing situation into an opportunity by giving this person special attention. For instance, I was once involved in a dinner for a candidate with a special guest speaker. It was a Monday night downtown at one of the nicer restaurants. We had called all of the people receiving invitations ahead of time and had an exact prepaid head count. On the night of the dinner, someone not on the list showed up. The woman checking people in at the door was scouring the list looking for this supporter's name.

I happened to notice what was going on and could clearly see the frustration and embarrassment on the guest's face as those behind waited and those in front looked back. I went over and said "Hello" to the supporter. Then turning to the woman checking in the names, I said that she probably would not find his name because I had failed to put it on the list. I then gave him my seat and leaned over and thanked him for his ongoing support. If his name was supposed to appear somewhere on the list, it didn't matter. It might have been there. The important thing was to remedy the uncomfortable situation at hand as quickly and gracefully as possible.

You never want to lose a supporter over a fund-raising meal. It costs the campaign almost nothing to keep this individual on-board. You must try to anticipate and avoid anything that might humiliate a person and leave a bad impression about a campaign. Take care of your supporters.

Holding a Special Event

A good rule of thumb for planning special events for fund-raising is that you need one week of preparation for every ten people you plan to attend. The preparation takes place in four stages.

1. You must define the purpose or purposes the event is to accomplish.

2. You must plan the event.

3. You must promote the event.

4. You must conduct the event.

Tips for handling each of these stages:

1. *Determine the purpose and type of event.*

Be clear on the purpose of the event. Is it to attract donors, raise money, raise support, thank volunteers and supporters, or just to get the word out on the measure or the candidate? Special events can, of course, have more than one purpose, but you need to focus on one purpose before you can pick the event. Focus on the main purpose when choosing the type of event; then see whether other purposes might be accomplished as well.

I have had great luck hosting dinners as fund-raising events. I contact a supportive restaurant and ask whether the owner will donate the dinner at cost in the restaurant. I then sell it to the guests at retail. Generally the restaurant can't afford the whole affair, so I go to another eatery and ask whether the owner will donate the dessert, and another for a donation of the coffee, wine, and so on. You can ask a local group to volunteer their talents for the music to make the occasion special. Restaurants are often closed on Mondays, making a perfect night for your fund-raiser.

I have also had great luck with intimate affairs at people's homes. This is different from a coffee and usually involves a well-known local providing a lavishly catered meal for a well-known candidate at a pretty hefty price. I try, in this scenario, to be selective about whom I invite, although usually the price will select who will attend, and the invitees know that. We have brought in as much as $6000 in our small area for this type of dinner.

I have found that coffees sponsored by a supporter can be a good special event. I will add, however, that they can also be a miserable failure. To avoid this they must, like all special events, be closely supervised to be successful. Since the campaign is not the sponsor, the critical factor is who hosts the coffee for you. If the sponsor is a local leader, such as a county commissioner, state representative, mayor, president of the college or university, a highly regarded business leader, philanthropist, or anyone with a following, there will be a good turn out. Most people do not like to go to political fund-raisers such as coffees, so the drawing card should be the combination of the candidate and the host of the coffee. Regardless who holds the coffee, the campaign should oversee the invitations and conduct the follow-up phone calls to ensure good attendance. A host who invites 60 people only to have 3 show up may feel humiliated because he or she let you down. Or the host may feel the candidate is responsible for the poor turn out. Either way, the candidate and the campaign manager have been deprived of one more night at home or time that could have been spent raising money by phone, preparing for a debate, or getting volunteers for a canvass.

"Every experienced campaigner knows that money follows hard work. It is not the other way around."

Margaret Sanger

Nothing is worse for the candidate than going to a poorly attended coffee, especially if you're already worried about winning. It is awful for the three supporters that do show up. Lending campaign support to ensure a successful coffee is time well spent.

Candidate Calls

If it's at all possible, have the candidate call the people invited to the coffee, or at least some of them. This will assure a donation if they are going, and if they can't make it, it is your opportunity to ask for money or support.

If you're going to have the candidate call, you can handle it something like this:

> *"Hello, Sam? Cathy Golden. Say, I just got a list of all the people invited to Shirley's coffee, and when I saw your name, I had to take a moment to call and tell you how much I am looking forward to you being there. It should be a lot of fun. Bring some tough questions for me, will you? Great, see you there."*

Using coffees effectively will bring you money, workers, and lawn-sign locations. So if you are going to host them, pay attention to the details and make each one as successful as possible.

Another good fund-raiser is an auction. You and your campaign team can go to businesses, supporters, whomever, and get a wide variety of donations. For example, you get four different video places to donate one children's movie, and then put them all together for one auction item. Your campaign volunteers can donate baked goods for the auction. It may work to have the candidate or the spouse be the auctioneer. I have used a popular local name who can really work the crowd. Be creative and you can have a fun event that actually brings in money. A good auction will bring in a minimum of $5000 in a small community.

If an auction is too much, how about a yard sale? If you're going to plan one, make it an event. Get a huge yard and lots of donations, old and new. Advertise the great stuff well in advance. Yard sales can be very good fund-raising events because almost no money is spent to set one up. An effective one will, however, take a lot of campaign committee and volunteer time to set up, run, and clean up after. Because a big yard sale can be grueling, be careful not to schedule one during other labor-intensive activities such as canvassing. A good yard sale can bring in $2000. Since most of the money comes in the first day, I strongly recommend you advertise it as one day only. Should you decide to do two days, cut the second day so it ends by 12:00 noon or 1:00 PM. Be sure to get some pizza for your volunteers at lunch. Use the proceeds of the yard sale.

Involve Attendees

One event I held in a small community was a dessert bake-off. I called specific supporters in that area and asked that they bring their very best desserts. I charged an entry fee for all but the bakers. The campaign provided the coffee (donated), and I involved other locals as the judges. I made up ribbons with different awards such as "Dessert Most Likely to Keep a Marriage Together," and each dessert won a prize. Because it was held in a small community, all who attended knew each other. Everyone had a great time, and other than the rental of the building, there were no costs to the campaign.

Whatever the type of event, a big consideration is the location. Is it big enough? Too big? How about the atmosphere? For indoor events, *never* use a huge hall or room, unless you are expecting a huge crowd. When selecting locations, I look for places where rooms can be closed off in case of poor attendance. No matter how many people come, I want the event to look like it is successful. You want people to have the impression that just the number invited and expected came. In selecting a restaurant for a dinner, try to find one that has a medium-sized room with another adjoining it that can be used or closed off as needed.

When choosing the type of event to have, you may want to consider your budget. Then, figure roughly what it will cost the campaign and what income it is likely to generate. You also need to estimate the commitment necessary from the candidate, the campaign team, and your volunteers. Don't forget to consider the economic climate in the community. A fifty-dollar-a-plate dinner in a town where the last factory just closed might not be a very good idea, even if it would make you money. When considering an event, always ask: Does this make sense? Does it fit? Does it feel right?

2. Plan the Event.

Planning an event is just an extension of choosing the event. All the considerations that informed your choice of the event must now be put into a plan. In other words, it is time to sort out the details. For instance, some events will require licenses or permits from local government. They can be a factor in deciding to hold an event, but once it is decided, someone has to make sure the permit is obtained. Similarly, the location, which was a factor in deciding on the type of event, must now be secured. The theme of the event, a human

"Nonpolitical issues are the most political."
Bill Meulemans

services luncheon, environmentalist dinner, or a school auction, now must influence the details of the event.

To run a successful special event, it is critical that you know who your audience is and how to reach it. For example, are you planning a library support dinner? If so, you need to get a mailing list from supportive groups.

Once you know whom you want to reach, you must decide how to reach them. Printed invitations with a phone call follow-up might work well for a formal dinner. If, however, the event is a yard sale, just advertise it in the paper or place flyers around town. Whatever the means, people must be assigned to accomplish it. Invitations must get printed. Flyers must be designed, printed, and distributed. Ads have to be written and delivered. All this takes time and people, and you will need to plan accordingly.

A good way to make sure the details are taken care of is to put the event on a time-line map, just like the one for the whole campaign, only smaller. Placing the event on a time-line and scheduling in all the tasks will require leadership—some *one* person needs to be in charge. That person needs to have volunteers assigned to all aspects of the event. Like the campaign itself, successful special events are the product of organization. If you assign the leadership of a special event to one person, provide ample volunteer help, develop a time-line, and plan a budget, you will have a successful event.

While budgets are an extra step, making one will not only help you get a handle on expenses but will remind you of things that need to be done. For example, listing the cost of the room expense may remind you to check the date of the event to see what else is going on in the community at that time. If you're hosting that dinner to support your town library, you don't want to find out right after you printed the invitations and rented the hall that it is on the same night as the homecoming game for your high school. Paying for the ads for your auction may remind you to see whether the hospital auction is on the same weekend. Here is a list of the things that could be included on a budget:

- *Site rental*
- *Drinks*
- *Printing*
- *Mailings*
- *Professionals*
- *Advertisements*
- *Insurance*
- *Use permits*
- *Clean-up*
- *Thank-you mailing*

- *Food*
- *Rental (sound system, tables, chairs)*
- *Supplies*
- *Entertainment*
- *Parking*
- *Decorations*
- *Fees*
- *Liquor licenses*
- *Awards, door prizes*

In planning your event, remember that, although someone in your organization is in charge, when it comes time to actually pulling it off, you may need to help, not only with volunteers, but with training. Training and staffing requirements must be met before the actual set-up begins.

In addition to having trained helpers available, you must plan for the supplies you will need. Often supplies must be ordered well ahead of the event. For instance, decorations may require lead time. These are the kind of things that go on your special event time line. Remember that things such as decorations that will cost you money are also in your special event budget. If you keep going back to the budget, or your expense list, it will remind you of things you might have forgotten.

Keep in mind, when planning an event, that some things won't show up on your budget or time line, but may nonetheless be critical. For instance, legal issues such as not being able to hold political events in public buildings must be considered. On the more mundane, but not less critical level, be sure to have duplicates of essential items. If a slide projector is necessary for an event, it is wise to have two projectors or at least two bulbs. How about extension cords or an extra microphone? While you're thinking about duplicates, how about duplicate lists of all the important phone numbers of the people you are depending on, such as the vendors, caterers, entertainers, staff, and volunteers. Maybe you will want to get a cellular phone for the event. Don't forget to acknowledge all sponsors and your volunteers.

3. Promote the Event.

To promote a special event properly, you must have a target audience in mind. Consider the income level and age of your target audience. Once you have that audience in mind, you must find some way to reach them. Your first job is to figure out where you are going to get lists of the people in your target audience. If you have a narrow group in mind, such as teachers, doctors, or human service advocates, you can often get mailing lists from the special interest groups these people belong to or support. If your audience is broader, as it would be for a neighborhood bake sale, you can take the list from a general source such as your county walking list.

Once you know whom you are trying to contact, you must decide how best to do it. Some possibilities are:
- *Invitations*
- *Flyers*
- *Radio and TV*
- *Press releases*
- *Posters*
- *Newsletters*

- *Handbills*
- *Calendars*
- *Word of mouth*

Whatever the vehicle you use to get your message out, the content and design must be attractive, professional, and clear. Include the date, place, time (beginning and end), cost, and clear directions for getting there. You need to include how much of the charge for the event is tax refundable. For instance, if the cost of the meal is $10 and you're charging $25, then $15 is tax deductible or refundable. Instead of putting the math in the ad, simply put a footnote at the bottom of the ad stating what amount of the price is deductible.

4. Conduct the Event.

When it is time to conduct a well-planned and promoted special event, the most important thing you can do to ensure success is to set up early. Everything should be ready 45 minutes to an hour early. As the organizer, you need to keep focused and calm. Your volunteers will take their cue from you, and that message must be calm efficiency. It is a nice touch to have a packet for volunteer organizers with their names on it. Include the overall plan, as well as the individual responsible for the volunteer.

Once people start to arrive, your focus should be on hospitality. How you greet people and work with them will set the tone of the event. Allow adequate time for the candidate to circulate. Do not schedule or allow, the candidate to "help" with the operation of the event. The candidate should not be doing things other than meeting the supporters. Name tags will help the candidate when greeting the guests.

Remember to thank everyone, even the people who sold you things. Everyone involved—volunteer, guest, or vendor—is forming an impression of the candidate and the campaign. You need to do everything you can to make a positive impression. That means a good clean-up, even if you have rented the facility, so make sure there are volunteers who will stay to clean-up. Never, as an organizer, leave people to clean up alone. Stay until it is done.

Candidate Calls to Raise Money

"The highest use of capital is not to make more money, but to make money do more for the betterment of life."

Henry Ford

Direct contact by the candidate remains the most effective, quickest, and cheapest way to raise money. It is critical to the success of a campaign. Remember, as the candidate, you are willing to do a job and volunteer your time at a task that few want to do. If people support your programs and ideas, they must show you by contributing to your campaign and thereby helping you get your name out. Do not sound apologetic. You are doing the community a favor.

As a campaign manager, I often call for moderate money and leave the calls for big money to my candidate. However, when I have been the candidate, I have made all the calls. It is very difficult for people to turn the candidate down, and I have found it to be time well spent. Set up some time each day to make the calls. It is helpful if the calls can be made from a prepared list that has phone numbers and suggests the amount to ask and the name to use.

Calling for Money for Ballot Measures

When fund-raising for ballot measures, it is sometimes easier to set up a goal for a specific item such as a full-page ad or TV buys. Let people know what you are trying to buy and how much it will cost so they can contribute accordingly.

If you are going to use a phone bank for fund-raising, use just a few people who are committed and identified in the community with the measure. Here is what you do:

1. Take your 5x8 card as described in the Volunteer section and head it: "Fund-raising." Place "Name," "Phone #," "CB?" and "Amount Pledged" across the top.

Activity: Fund-raising			
NAME	PHONE #	CB?	AMOUNT PLEDGED

Fig. 4.1 Example of Fund-raising Activity Card

2. List the people you want to call and their phone numbers.

3. When you call, let them know what they are buying. For example, I

might tell people that I am trying to raise $1500 for a last minute ad campaign and ask what they can give toward it.

4.   Whatever they say, I place that amount under the "Amount" column.

5.   People prefer to sign on to something that's going to fly, so I will tell potential donors that we are "X" dollars away our goal.

6.   The campaign should decide whether contributors will send the check to you or the treasurer. In a pledge situation such as this, I have done it both ways, although I like it better when they send the check to me directly. In this way I can keep track of who sent their pledges in for a follow-up phone call.

7.   Either way, if the check is not in to the campaign within a week, make a quick reminder call and note it in the "CB?" column.

Your fund-raising will go a lot better, particularly in a small town or county, if you NEVER (look as though you are) SPEND(ing) MORE MONEY THAN YOU HAVE. That is to say, never spend more money than you have and never *look* as though you are spending more money than you have. Voters do not look favorably on candidates who cannot live within their fund-raising abilities.

One thing I do to be sure this does not happen is to set up business accounts everywhere. Newspapers require that campaign advertising be paid before the ad runs, but printers, typesetters, small newspapers, and other vendors will allow you to run an account and pay with one check at the end of the campaign. While the money is technically spent, it does not show up as such when you are filing your C&E report. Setting up accounts around town means printing fewer checks, which can also save you money. I usually get by on a small election with bank-issued dummy checks alone.

"Big money brings big problems."
    Bill Meulemans

Chapter 5

Lawn Signs

In this chapter

Logo and General Information

Location, Location, Location

Preparing for the First Day

Big Signs

Maintenance of Signs

Lawn-Sign Removal

Lawn sign placement/maintenance is a great place to involve people who are not interested in interfacing with the public (or people you feel might make an unfavorable impression). It is not a huge time commitment if you have enough volunteers, and it can be very gratifying. In my town, lawn signs cannot be placed more than 30 days prior to an election. I therefore have everything prepared for the big day when all the signs suddenly appear.

Let me digress a moment. There are two schools of thought here. One is to not worry if you do not have a lot of locations at first since it is what you end up with that counts. This opinion argues that what is important is the appearance of *building* momentum. The other school of thought is that BOOM! here comes the candidate. Suddenly the name is out, and everyone supports that person. I am of the latter school. I work like crazy to get as many locations as possible for the big day. I do this obviously to make a big visual impact, but also because I only have to organize the signs going up once. I know that there will always be additional requests as the campaign goes on, but not so many that one or two people can't handle them in each city. I always have volunteers whose sole job in the campaign is to put up lawn signs as people call and ask for them or as canvassers secure the new locations.

As I stated before, I have everything ready and organized for my teams. Also note that it is especially important that people work in pairs in this activity: one to drive the car or truck and the other to hop out and pound.

Logo and General Information

For the purposes of this handbook, a logo is your name or ballot measure and a message written in a memorable way. Sometimes the name will be written with a star and streamers behind it, or a wavy American flag, or stars and stripes. I had one that was quite blocky with the name written in different colored bars. I did another one that was fairly complicated with a backdrop of the city, trees, clouds, anchovies, the works. Because I have no imagination and even less talent in these areas, I take this task to a professional. The going rate for developing a logo in my area is $100. Since you will be looking at your logo for months, take a little time here. It is money well spent.

Lawn signs, like all advertising, must easily identify your cause or candidate. You need to develop your own "look." Once you have a logo, try to use it in all campaign literature and advertising. If you or your campaign team do not have the skills, you will have to use a graphic design artist or a typesetter to design your name logo.

Regardless of who does your signs and logo, it is a good idea to visit a lawn-sign printer. They usually save at least one of each of the signs that they have ever printed. This way you can shop for ideas in style and color combinations without any out-of-pocket expenses. When you're designing your sign, keep in mind that two colors cost a lot more than one, but they're worth it. To save some money, you can get a two (or even three) color look by doing almost a solid color over the stock while leaving the lettering with no color. This produces white lettering on what looks like colored stock. Then use half tones (a mix of the white sign and the solid color showing through) for a design or part of the lettering. Very classy.

Weatherproof Stock

Even if money is a big problem, *do not cut costs on your stock*. Get good paper stock that is weatherproof. Something like poly tag or corrugated works well. The corrugated stock is nice because it is printed on both sides of the same sign, thus eliminating the need to staple signs back-to-back. Stapled signs often come apart and need repair. Also, corrugated can be attached to the stake prior to pounding it in the ground. (Be sure to use screws and washers.)

If you are using poly tag, remember to bring in your clerical team to staple the signs back-to-back. This needs to be done prior to placing the signs in yards. *Do not attach poly tag signs to the stakes prior to pounding the stakes in the ground. THEY WILL FALL OFF!*

Have the signs and the stakes bound together in groups of 25. If you have the signs and stakes already counted, you need only assign the area and direct the team to take the appropriate number of bundles of stakes and signs.

Remember, anything that is not weatherproof will curl with the first strong dew or rain, and your campaign "look" will be one of litter. Political lawn signs are a touchy subject in some communities. Keep lawn signs neat and together at all times. If you're sloppy about quality, placement, or maintenance, lawn signs may do more harm than good. But, if you do it right, they make your campaign look well organized and staffed.

Stakes for lawn signs are expensive. To save money, I ask other campaigns to give me their stakes after elections. I then bundle the stakes in sets of 25 and redistribute to campaigns I support. Call around to those who have run and lost or are not running again and collect stakes. This works especially well if you are running a single campaign in the fall and someone you know lost in the primary election. If you have no luck, try to get a secondary wood products company or nursery to donate them. Still no luck? Ask supporters in the construction industry to make you some. Still no luck? Swallow hard and buy them. You can count on your lawn signs plus stakes costing $2 each. Budget accordingly, and place them carefully. Plan on buying 3–4 foot stakes.

If you are endorsed by fire fighters or some other well-organized group, they may have the ability to print lawn signs with some limitations, such as numbers of colors or size. Check out such groups; it could save you money.

Halloween

If you're running a fall campaign, you should be prepared to send all of your lawn-sign workforce back out the day after Halloween. It is just a few days before the fall general election date in November. You want your campaign to look great right up to the end. Extra effort and foresight are not lost on the electorate, nor are the opposite traits. I know this may sound obvious, but be sure the signs are put up perpendicular to the street. The point of lawn signs is for people to see them from a distance as they drive by.

To get any benefit from lawn signs, you need to attract the attention of voters. Your "look" and how you present it will determine the success of lawn signs. In a mayoral race some years ago, an outsider ran a really great lawn-sign campaign. One of the most distinguishing marks of his campaign was small, undersized lawn signs that he used in place of the normal-sized signs. Neighborhoods began having competitions to see who had the most signs up. Some houses would have ten of these signs on the front lawn. In some areas, neighbors would try to get their entire block to be covered with the "cute" little lawn signs. Meanwhile, the opponent ran a very traditional campaign using only billboards, and, needless to say, lost. Don't hesitate to be creative and bold. You never know what will work. Bold, however, does not mean elaborate. Simple signs with a simple theme are the least offensive and easiest to read at high speeds.

Location, Location, Location

Getting good locations to display your signs is the second half of using lawn signs effectively. One way to find good locations is to ask for locations from other campaigns who are not running. Another way is to get a "walking list" (list of addressees within a particular voting district) for your district from the county clerk. Using a map and this list, note the arterial streets. You can then set up a phone bank to call people living on the favored arterial and ask whether they will allow you to place a lawn sign on their property. This really works.

If the walking lists from the county do not have many phone numbers, set up a clerical team to come in and look up phone numbers ahead of the phone bank. The idea of having a system for organizing volunteers is that you can quickly bring groups of people to bear on problems. Organization allows you to accomplish tasks without overloading your workers.

Many times people who have run for office in previous elections will have records of where their lawn signs were placed. Try to get such lists and call them first. This works best when you share political ideology with a former candidate.

When possible, try to avoid placing your sign where many lawn signs have already been placed. Give high priority to placement of signs in yards of people registered in the opposite party or where there are lawn signs of people running in another race in the opposite party. This gives voter the impression that you are supported by a wide cross section of your community.

Preparing for the First Day

Setting up for placing lawn signs follows the same process as the other campaign activities we have talked about. After getting locations and making sure that the posters and stakes are ready to go, you now need to organize the team that will put up the signs.

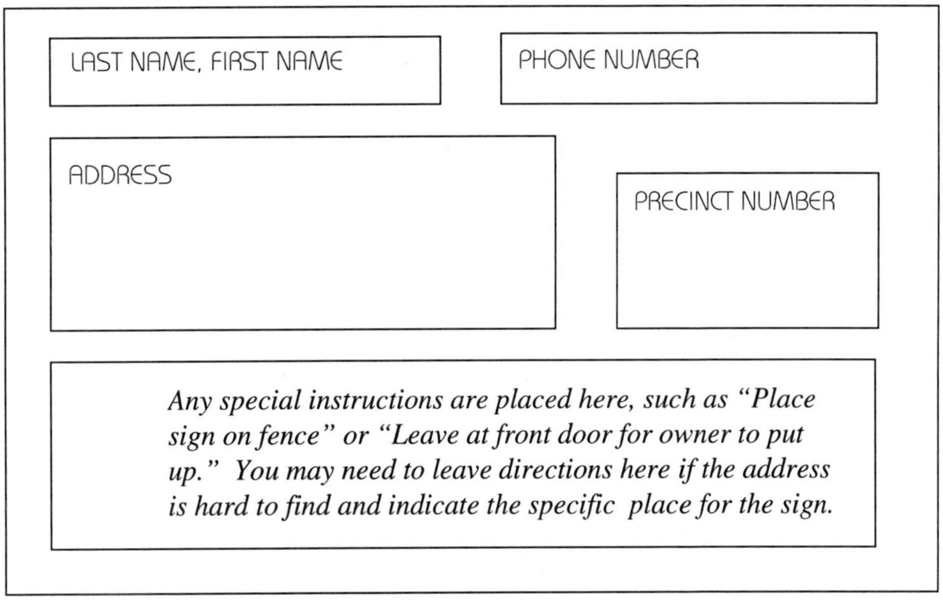

```
┌─────────────────────────────────────────────────────┐
│  LAST NAME, FIRST NAME        PHONE NUMBER            │
│                                                       │
│  ADDRESS                                              │
│                               PRECINCT NUMBER         │
│                                                       │
│                                                       │
│     Any special instructions are placed here, such    │
│     as "Place sign on fence" or "Leave at front door  │
│     for owner to put up." You may need to leave       │
│     directions here if the address is hard to find    │
│     and indicate the specific place for the sign.     │
└─────────────────────────────────────────────────────┘
```

Fig. 5.1 Example of 3x5 Lawn Sign Card

Begin by placing all of your lawn sign locations on 3x5 cards as shown above. Once the cards are filled out, organize them by addresses that are close to each other. Use maps or people who know the neighborhood. If you cannot find a street on the map, call the home for a location. What you are after is some kind of logical walking or driving pattern that will allow your placement team to save time and motion. I use groupings of no more than 20–30 locations. Each will take about two hours.

After you have the 3x5 location cards organized, place the cards for each grouping in a ziplock baggy along with a map with the target area highlighted. Set these baggies aside for your placement crews.

Placement crews work in two's. If you are using poly tag, the crew needs a staple gun (to attach the sign to the stake), a stapler (in case the sign comes apart at the corners), and a mallet to pound the stake into the ground. If they are placing corrugated signs, they will need only a mallet and maybe a metal pole to use for making a pilot hole. In either case, it is a good idea to bring along extra signs or repair kits (washers, screws, electric screwdrivers, staple guns, staples, stakes, mallets) in case a sign breaks. If you are using something other than either of these types of signs, just remember, send extras of everything.

Assigning crews is then simply a matter of handing them a baggy with the locations on 3x5 cards plus a map highlighted with their area and the appropriate number of signs and stakes. Ask as many volunteers as possible to bring tools or borrow enough ahead of time from friends. Be sure everything borrowed by the campaign is labeled and returned promptly.

It is also critical that the volunteer brings back the baggy with the 3x5 cards. You will need your cards for the maintenance crews to repair signs after Halloween and for sign pick-up at the end of the election.

I am a firm believer that poorly constructed, poorly designed lawn signs hurt your campaign more than they help. If you are going to do lawn signs, they are way too expensive and too labor intensive to cut corners on design and production. If you can't raise the money to do them right, don't do them.

With that said, there may be times when you deviate from this rule for strategic reasons. In one campaign, due to lack of funds, we printed only one-third the normal number of lawn signs. Although they were carefully placed to maximize visibility, they soon began to disappear. People were calling wanting signs; others were calling requesting replacements. We knew it was a close race and our diminishing number of signs looked as though support was waning.

So using the same color of ink as our signs, I hand painted more in my barn on the back of old lawn-sign stock. In the middle of the night I placed them throughout the city. I did not want these to be next to each other, but rather to lend the impression that the homeowner had taken the initiative to paint a sign. I wanted the look to be one of individual, rebellious support for our side and angry opposition to the money fighting our effort.

Big Signs

Large signs placed along highways can be very effective advertising. I have worked on campaigns where large signs have been painted by hand and others where they were commercially printed. Naturally, such signs are not cheap. My preference is to have volunteers paint them for free, but that is a lot to ask of anyone because it is so time consuming. I would add here that this can be a little touchy if the hand-painted signs end up looking amateurish and you feel placement would be problematic for the campaign. However they are produced, location is the primary concern when using large signs.

Large sign locations can sometimes be found by calling realtors who have parcels listed along highways and in cities. Ranchers, farmers, or owners of large vacant lots who support you will occasionally allow signs on the corners of their land. If you're running a local campaign during a general election, talk to state or even national campaigns about possible large sign locations near theirs.

The volunteer crew putting up large signs must be carefully selected. They should have some construction experience so the structure can withstand wind and the weight of the sign. They will need more than a hammer and nails to put up a large sign. Supply them with or ask them to bring post-hole diggers, shovels, hammers, nails, and additional wood for supports or bracing. This is a big production.

Maintenance of Signs

Large or small, campaign signs must be maintained once they are up. Depending on the circumstances, you may use the same crew that placed the signs to maintain them throughout the campaign, or you may use a completely different crew. Whomever you use, they must travel with a mallet, staple gun, extra signs, stakes, stapler, and so on in their cars at all times. Ostensibly, maintenance crews are ready for repair of any ailing sign they see in their normal daily travels. However, from time to time there may be a need for the crews to travel their assigned placement routes for a more systematic check of the signs.

As I indicated before, you will need to keep your maps and baggies of 3x5 lawn sign location cards for your maintenance crews, for post-Halloween repairs, and for sign removal after the election. As well as hanging onto the cards, I keep all lawn-sign locations in my computer. That way I can print sections of the lawn sign list as I need them to give to the maintenance people. Before I computerized, in addition to my 3x5 cards, I kept the locations handwritten on paper according to area. I then photocopied these lists for maintenance people. If you do not have an organized maintenance crew, you will need these lists only for the day after Halloween or after a severe storm.

Besides maintenance, there will be the chore of putting up new signs as people call in requesting them or as canvassers return with requests for lawn signs. If there aren't too many, you can assign new locations to the appropriate maintenance crew or have special volunteers to do this chore on an ongoing basis.

In one campaign with which I was involved, there was a street where every night all of the lawn signs disappeared. The man who put the signs in that area was also in charge of maintenance and just happened to drive this street to and from work each day. After the signs disappeared and were replaced a couple of times, the volunteer decided to take them down on his way home from work and then each morning on the way to work put them back up. You can't buy that kind of loyalty.

It is best to get requested signs up as soon as possible. However, if there are too many, it may be necessary to organize another day for placement.

If you do this, be sure to include all of your current locations so that signs can be repaired or replaced if missing.

Lawn-Sign Removal

Most localities have regulations about removing campaign signs. Regardless, your crews should be ready to remove all of your lawn signs the day after the election. If left up longer, homeowners begin to take signs in and even throw them away, and you won't have them for your next election. At a minimum, you will want to retrieve the stakes for future campaigns. Since you have to get them down eventually, you might as well look organized and responsible by getting them as quickly as possible.

I like to set up a crew for the day after the election. Again, I work volunteers in pairs and give these crews maps and the 3x5 cards containing the addresses. When they return, you must remember to get your cards and maps back for the next election. This is also a great time to get together a volunteer thank-you party to disassemble your lawn signs, put them away for the next election, and bundle your stakes in sets of 25 with duct tape.

Chapter 6

Precinct Analysis:

The Sinners, the Saints, and the Saveables

In this chapter

The Full-blown Analysis
The Quick and Dirty Precinct Analysis
Forms

If you intend to canvass or run a get-out-the-vote effort, you must do a voter precinct analysis. If you have money, you may hire a voter contact service to do it for you. If not, read this section carefully. You will need a precinct analysis in order to determine where best to invest your money, time, and especially your canvassing efforts. Unlike some campaign activities, precinct analysis is something that can be done months ahead of the election. Take advantage of this and get it out of the way.

Precinct analysis is based on the premise that people who think and vote alike live near each other. Precinct analysis looks for voting trends, specifically precinct-by-precinct voting trends, which indicate high support and low voter turnout for similar candidates or causes in past elections. In every race, a candidate or cause will find three types of voters:

The Sinners. These are the voters that will not cast a vote your way regardless of what you say or do. In fact, you *never* want to give them a reason to get out to vote. You do not canvass them and hope they will forget to turn out on election day.

"Aim at the souls that can be saved."
Bill Meulemans

The Saints. Those who will vote for you over your opponent almost no matter what. If these voters turn out in record numbers, they need little attention in the campaign. If you spend time and money here, you are preaching to the choir.

The Saveables. Those who will or are inclined to vote for your cause if you can just turn them out to vote.

Once you have this information, you can send your campaign volunteers into the area of the saveables and try to activate those people to vote for your cause. That is called canvassing, and it is effective only after you have done a precinct analysis.

The Full-blown Analysis

The precinct analysis is a little different for a primary than for a general election. In a primary, candidates of the same party square off, and so the analysis is made of past voting records for candidates of that particular party. For the general, you are comparing past voting trends of all parties voting if the election is for a candidate. If it is for a ballot measure, you are comparing voting histories for similar ballot measures or propositions. In either case, the materials you need in order to do a precinct analysis are the same regardless of the type of election. To do a precinct analysis, you will need the county printouts of the identified elections and a number of copies of the forms found in this chapter. Typically, depending on the size of the area you are analyzing, you will need one to five copies of the Election Data Form 1, found in the "Forms" section at the end of this handbook, one copy of the Precinct Targeting Worksheet (*Form 2*) and the Precinct Priorities Worksheet (*Form 3*), and three copies of the Targeting Priorities & Strategy Worksheet (*Form 4*).

You start your precinct analysis by researching past local elections that were similar to the one you are working on. Be as specific as you can about elections. For example, was the election:
- *A school board election with a liberal vs. a conservative?*
- *A county commission race between two conservative Democrats?*
- *A county commission race between two liberal Republicans?*
- *A liberal Republican vs. a conservative Democrat?*
- *A primary election between a man and a woman?*
- *An incumbent vs. outsider general election?*
- *School tax levies?*
- *Bond levies for construction of swimming pools?*
- *County-wide tax base*

Whatever the combination of your particular candidates or ballot measure, find a past election with a similar combination.

Once you have identified the appropriate past election(s), go to the county election office and request a printout of the particular race or races that you've identified. Bring home the printouts and set aside a couple of hours to work with the precinct analysis forms. First, you need to make enough copies of the Election Data Form 1 to cover the number of precincts involved in the election. Each copy of the Election Data Form will hold 22 precincts. Be sure to retain the original of the Election Data Form for future use. Fill it out according to the example shown in Fig. 6.1.

Election Data Form

Your analysis begins by going through the printout to get the information necessary to complete the Election Data Form 1 (see example *Fig. 6.1*). You will notice that the county printout includes more information than you need. Ignore the information that does not pertain to the race or races you have identified for analysis. Just go to the candidate or issue of interest on the printout and transfer that information to Election Data Form.

On Scratch Paper

Next, on a separate piece of paper, arrange the precincts in order of support *(see example Fig. 6.2)*. Transfer the precinct numbers to the Precinct Targeting Worksheet, Form 2 in the Forms section. See the example in Fig. 6.3. Make a copy of Form 2, if you haven't already done so, and retain the original for future use.

Precinct Targeting Worksheet

To fill out the Precinct Targeting Worksheet, you need to decide what constitutes high support for the issue or candidate you have selected as a model for your race. It might be a win of 60%, or it might be a win of only 52%. This can be a tough call. What you are looking for is the best support comparatively speaking for that particular election.

The best support may not necessarily be overwhelming support. I once worked on a campaign effort to defend an office holder against a recall attempt. The only other recall of a county commissioner in our area was 10 years prior. Since this previously recalled county commissioner had a similar ideology as my candidate, I did a precinct analysis based on the outcome of that election. Once I got the abstracts, I could see that the analysis would be very difficult. Not only had the precincts changed with the census, but the commissioner had been voted out about two-to-one. Finding *any* precincts with a win for the commissioner, much less "high" support, was next to impossible. Therefore, I adjusted the curve so that precincts where the official *kept* her office or was only *narrowly* recalled were considered "high" support. Medium support was adjusted also. For purposes of this analysis, the medium support areas consisted of precincts where she had been recalled, but not in overwhelming numbers. Low support areas were just those precincts where she was recalled in huge numbers.

In a similar way, you may adjust what you would consider high, medium, or low support areas. In other words, you are breaking out the precincts where the issue or candidate that is representative of your issue or candidate has done well, fairly well, or poorly. On the Precinct Targeting Worksheet, Form 2 (see example *Fig. 6.3*), on the left-hand side, list the precincts you have selected according to the appropriate category of support.

Now that you know where your support is likely to come from, you must identify precincts with high, moderate, and low voter *turnout*, that is, the percentage of registered voters who actually voted. To determine this, I divide the difference between the highest precinct turnout and the lowest into thirds. For example, if the lowest precinct turnout in the election was 25% and the highest was 75%, my high, moderate, and low turnout categories would be: high turnout, 60% and higher; moderate turnout, 45% to 59%; and low turnout, 44% and lower. List the results of your voter turnout analysis on the right-hand side of the Precinct Targeting Worksheet (see example *Fig. 6.3*) by category, just as you did for support.

Precinct Priorities Worksheet

Remember, you are making this step-by-step analysis to know where best to spend money and time. Once you have support and turnout broken out on the Precinct Targeting Worksheet, Form 2, go to the Precinct Priorities Worksheet, Form 3 (see example *Fig. 6.4*). As with the others, make a copy of the form and retain the original. The Precinct Priorities Worksheet, Form 3, is where you will be listing the precincts from highest to lowest priority for canvassing or getting out the vote. This is accomplished by simply matching high support and low turnout precincts from the Precinct Targeting Worksheet, Form 2 (see example *Fig. 6.3*) to establish your priority list. For example, all precincts that fall in both high support *and* low turnout categories on the Precinct Targeting Worksheet, Form 2 (see example *Fig. 6.3*) get placed in the first, or "highest priority" box of the Precinct Priorities Worksheet, Form 3, (see example *Fig. 6.4*). Those with low support and high turnout are the lowest priority. Other precincts will fall in-between on support or turnout and will end in the second box of the Precinct Priorities Worksheet, Form 3 (see example *Fig. 6.4*).

Targeting Priorities and Strategy Worksheet

You are now ready to take the first of your three copies of the Targeting Priorities & Strategy Worksheet, Form 4 (see example *Fig. 6.5*) and list all the number one precincts on that form. List the moderate priority precincts on the second sheet. On the third sheet, list your lowest priority precincts. You can now assign your canvass or get-out-the-vote teams where they will do the most good. High priority gets done first, then moderate priority. Leave low priority alone.

You may want to look over the lowest priority precincts and pull out the marginal ones for a *possible* canvass, but I usually avoid these precincts. Although these are not necessarily the sinners, they tend to vote for the *opposition*. Low-priority precincts are just that: low priority. Similarly, if you have high support and high turnout already, you have to ask yourself what your canvassing is likely to accomplish. These are the saints. With limited money, time, and volunteers, do you want to spend time where you already have the vote?

I once worked for a candidate who did not believe in precinct analysis. I had conducted an in-depth precinct analysis of a number of elections where there were candidates seeking office who embraced a similar political ideology as my candidate. I also reviewed initiatives that covered issues similar to ones with which my candidate was closely aligned. It was clear from the analysis that a handful of precincts would not support this candidate, and I told him which ones they were. These precincts were off limits because they came in as both low support and low turnout.

Notwithstanding the warning, toward the end of the campaign (with all the #1 and #2 precincts done), the candidate decided to burn up some restless energy by covering these low-priority precincts. His feeling was that if *he* personally went to the door, people would be swayed. My concern was that these low turnout precincts would turn out in higher than usual numbers and would not vote the way we needed. The candidate disagreed and went ahead with canvassing low-priority precincts.

The low-support precincts, not surprisingly, turned out to be difficult canvasses. People were rude, and mishaps occurred. The candidate came back demoralized but decided to press on.

Following the election I did a precinct analysis, and it showed that the low-priority precincts had turned out in huge numbers and voted two-to-one against my candidate. Given that we lost by only a few hundred votes, it might have swung the election our way had some of these people stayed home.

Swing Voters

If your precinct analysis is being done for a partisan race in a general election, you now need to find the swing voters. Swing voters are voters who are registered in one party, but will vote for someone from another party. Swing voters are also called "smart voters" because they vote according to issues and information rather than party. Your job is to find them and persuade them that they should jump party ranks and vote for your candidate.

To find your swing voters, get the voting printout for general elections with candidates similar to the campaign you are working on. Look through the printout for precincts with high Republican registration if you're working for a Democrat, or high Democrat registration if you're working for a Republican. This information is recorded on the Swing Voter Form 6 (see example *Fig. 6.6*). Make the necessary copies of the form according to the number of precincts.

For each precinct you've identified as high, medium, or low priority from your analysis, fill in the precinct number from #1 priority down, the number of registered voters, the number of registered Democrats, and the percentage of Democrats for that precinct. Do the same for Republicans. Also, record by precinct the percent yes votes for the candidate most like yours and the percent no for those voting for the opposition in the comparative election. Once you have all the information recorded on the Swing Voter Form 6 (see example *Fig. 6.6*), your mission is to look for precincts where the vote did not follow party lines. If you find precincts where large numbers of one party voted for the other party, take advantage of this with direct mail or canvassing. Don't worry about the turnout.

Undervote

Another thing to look for in precinct analysis is the undervote. The undervote represents voters who go to the polls or return a ballot but skip voting for a particular candidate or issue on their card. Undervotes may result from a candidate running unopposed, or because the voter didn't like any of the choices, or because the voter knows nothing about an issue or candidate and decides to leave the decision to those who do. The reasons for high undervotes are of interest in shaping a campaign and the campaign message. If they happen in high-priority precincts, it may be a good idea to put the candidate in for the canvass. You don't want your candidate or issue to be unknown in precincts where there is likely to be support.

I once worked for a candidate who ran uncontested in the primary. I came on board with his campaign in the general election because I had been involved in a different campaign during the primary. The candidate had decided that since he was unopposed in the primary he would not spend money during the primary. He was betting he could make the campaign happen in the general alone.

After the primary I did an analysis of the primary vote for both my candidate and the general election opponent. The analysis revealed that the opposing candidate, who also was uncontested but ran a modest primary campaign, had a relatively small undervote. My candidate, with no primary campaign at all, had undervotes that went as high as 60%. The high undervote may have been the result of the perception that the voters thought the candidate was "aloof" and somehow thought he was too good to campaign. Being invisible during the primary only fed this belief. We corrected this with canvassing prior to the general, but it is important to run a primary election campaign regardless of the opposition. You can make use of an opportunity to present the candidate to the voters as a sincere person who genuinely wants their votes.

Ballot Measure Form

To conduct a precinct analysis for a ballot measure, follow the example in *Figure 6.7*. As with any other precinct analysis, you must find an election that was similar to the one you are working on. Don't worry about party affiliation and do everything else as with a candidate precinct analysis.

The Quick and Dirty Precinct Analysis

If you do not have the time for an in-depth precinct analysis, there is a "quick and dirty" way to do one. This method will not give you the kind of information that the full analysis will, but if you are doing just a single city or school district, it works pretty well. As with the full-blown version, you must research similar elections to find a voting pattern. Once you have identified the races you are interested in, call the county and ask for the "summary sheets" or the printouts for those elections. Summary sheets are usually compiled by the county for all elections and list only the vote for, against, and the turnout by precinct. Most counties will fax these sheets to you. If not, ask for copies and pick them up at the courthouse.

To do your analysis, take a yellow highlighter and go through the summary looking for precincts that voted correctly (likely to support your cause) but had a low voter turnout. These precincts are your #1 priority. Once you have your high-priority precincts, look for precincts that show support with a medium or high turnout. These will be on your moderate list. If you see precincts where you are likely to lose big, just avoid them.

Using a Computer

If you have access to a data spreadsheet program in your computer you can save a great deal of time at the adding machine or calculator if you do the following.

For the Ballot Measure Form, create a spread sheet with at least nine columns. List from left to right:

Precinct Number
Location
Yes
No
Registered Voters
Turnout
% Turnout
% Yes
% No

From the county records data input the first four columns and then have the computer compute the last three in the following way:

- *for % turnout: divide turnout by registered voters*
- *for % yes: divide yes votes by turnout*
- *for % no: divide no votes by turnout.*

For the Election Data Form do the same, except adjust columns according to the enclosed form and have the computer compute the % columns in the following way:

- *% Democrats: divide registered Dem. by registered voters*
- *% Republicans: divide registered Rep. by registered voters*
- *% party turnout: divide turnout by the respective party registration number*
- *% support: divide individual candidate support by the respective party turnout.*

Forms

The following six pages show examples of completed forms and worksheets. "Elle Daniels" is the Republican candidate. Blank forms for your use are included in the Forms section at the end of this handbook.

Fig. 6.1 Example of Form 1

ELECTION DATA FORM

Candidate *Elle Daniels*   **County** *Grant*

Election Date *Primary, 1980*   **Page** *1* **of** *1* **Pages**

*T/O = Turnout   U/V = Undervote

Pre-cinct	Reg. Voters	Reg. Demos.		Dem. T/O	Reg. Repubs.		Rep. T/O		Nelson (D)		Com-stock (R)		Daniels (R)		Dem. U/V	Rep. U/V
01	1,366	710	52%	64%	529	39%	65%		55%		19%		66%	2nd	45%	14%
02	820	452	55%	69%	296	36%	72%		51%		19%		64%	4th	49%	17%
03	772	456	59%	54%	228	30%	56%		56%		30%		57%		44%	11%
04	698	380	54%	59%	247	35%	64%		57%		22%		69%	1st	43%	8%
05	900	494	55%	64%	313	35%	65%		58%		26%		56%		42%	18%
06	871	529	61%	57%	244	28%	59%		57%		21%		56%		43%	23%
07	497	313	63%	38%	125	25%	43%		57%		31%		59%		43%	9%
08	770	332	43%	65%	384	50%	72%		64%	1st	26%		65%	3rd	36%	10%
09	930	494	53%	57%	341	37%	62%		63%	2nd	39%	4th	53%		37%	8%
10	606	301	50%	65%	240	40%	62%		60%	5th	30%		59%		40%	11%
11	1,219	600	49%	59%	478	39%	68%		49%		44%	1st	46%		51%	10%
12	1,139	568	50%	61%	432	38%	67%		50%		22%		64%	5th	50%	14%
13	107	49	46%	53%	30	28%	70%		62%	4th	14%		52%		38%	33%
14	121	39	32%	69%	61	50%	54%		59%		42%	2nd	36%		41%	21%
15	368	234	64%	61%	92	25%	77%		52%		39%	5th	51%		48%	10%
16	225	146	65%	48%	60	27%	72%		51%		42%	3rd	37%		49%	21%
17	836	467	56%	60%	287	34%	61%		54%		32%		49%		46%	19%
18	499	316	63%	51%	148	30%	61%		58%		35%		51%		42%	14%
19	729	380	52%	57%	254	35%	60%		58%		38%		40%		42%	22%
20	982	590	60%	57%	287	29%	60%		63%	3rd	29%		58%		37%	13%
21	1,041	519	50%	58%	420	40%	66%		59%		34%		53%		41%	12%
22	283	127	45%	50%	134	47%	63%		52%		38%		52%		48%	11%

Fig. 6.2 Example

[On a sheet of scratch paper]

Arrange Precincts in
Declining Order of Support

Daniels Support			Republican Turnout		
04	69%		15	77%	
01	66%		02	72%	
08	65%	(5)	08	72%	(5)
02	64%		16	72%	
12	64%		13	70%	
07	59%		11	68%	
10	59%		12	67%	
20	58%		21	66%	
03	57%		01	65%	
05	56%	(10)	05	65%	(11)
06	56%		04	64%	
09	53%		22	63%	
21	53%		19	62%	
13	52%		10	62%	
22	52%		17	61%	
			18	61%	
15	51%				
18	51%		19	60%	
17	49%	(7)	20	60%	
11	46%		06	59%	
19	40%		03	56%	(6)
16	37%		14	54%	
14	36%		07	43%	

Fig. 6.3 Example of Form 2

PRECINCT TARGETING WORKSHEET

* High Support   ** High Turnout

H/S* Support	H/T** Turnout
(04)	15
01	02
08	08
02	16
12	13

M/S	M/T
07	11
10	12
20	21
03	01
05	05
06	(04)
09	22
21	09
13	10
22	17
	18

L/S	L/T
15	19
18	20
17	06
11	03
19	14
16	07
14	

Fig. 6.4 Example of Form 3

PRECINCT PRIORITIES WORKSHEET

(1) H/S + L/T = High Priority	(6) M/S + H/T = Medium Priority *13*
(2) H/S + M/T = High Priority *(04)* *01* *12*	(7) L/S + L/T = Low Priority *19* *14*
(3) M/S + L/T = High Priority *07* *20* *03* *06*	(8) L/S + M/T = Low Priority *18* *17* *11*
(4) M/S + M/T = Medium Priority *10* *05* *09* *21* *22*	(9) L/S + H/T = Low Priority *15* *16*
(5) H/S + H/T = Medium Priority *08* *02*	

*Fig. 6.5 Example
of Form 4*

TARGETING PRIORITIES & STRATEGY FORM

Rep.   Daniels   Rep.   Rep.

Prio-rity	Pre-cinct	Reg. Voters	Party Density	Support	T/O	U/V	Precinct Location	Campaign Strategy
2	04	698	35%	69%	64%	8%	*Hills*	*Athletic canvassers*
2	01	1,366	39%	66%	65%	14%		
2	12	1,139	38%	64%	67%	14%		*Senior canvassers*
3	07	497	25%	59%	43%	9%		
3	20	982	29%	58%	60%	13%		
3	03	772	30%	57%	56%	11%		
3	06	871	28%	56%	59%	23%		*Candidate canvasses*
4	10	301	40%	59%	62%	11%		*(etc.)*
4	05	900	35%	56%	65%	18%		
4	09	930	37%	53%	62%	8%		
4	21	1,041	40%	53%	66%	12%		
4	22	283	47%	52%	63%	11%		
5	08	770	50%	65%	72%	10%		
5	02	820	36%	64%	72%	17%		
6	13	107	28%	52%	70%	33%		
7	19	729	35%	40%	60%	22%		
7	14	121	50%	36%	54%	21%		
8	18	499	30%	51%	61%	14%		
8	17	836	34%	49%	61%	19%		
8	11	1,219	39%	46%	68%	10%		
9	15	368	25%	51%	77%	10%		
9	16	225	48%	37%	72%	21%		

*HIGH
(7)*

*MED.
(8)*

*LOW
(7)*

Fig. 6.6 Example
of Form 6

SWING VOTERS FORM

	Priority	Precinct	Reg. Voters	Reg. Demos.	% Demo. Party Density	Reg. Repubs.	% Repub. Party Density	Support Yes	Support No
HIGH (7)	2	04	698	710	52	529	39	69%	31
	2	01	1,366	452	55	296	36	66%	34
	2	12	1,139	456	59	228	30	64%	36
	3	07	497	380	54	247	35	59%	41
	3	20	982	494	55	313	35	58%	42
	3	03	772	529	61	244	28	57%	43
	3	06	871	313	63	125	25	56%	44
MED. (8)	4	10	301	332	43	384	50	59%	41
	4	05	900	494	65	341	37	56%	44
	4	09	930	301	50	240	40	53%	47
	4	21	1,041	600	49	478	39	53%	47
	4	22	283	568	50	432	38	52%	48
	5	08	770	49	46	30	28	65%	35
	5	02	820	39	32	61	50	64%	36
	6	13	107	234	64	92	25	52%	48
LOW (7)	7	19	729	146	65	60	27	40%	60
	7	14	121	467	56	287	34	36%	64
	8	18	499	316	63	148	30	51%	49
	8	17	836	380	52	254	35	49%	51
	8	11	1,219	590	60	287	29	46%	54
	9	15	368	519	50	420	40	51%	49
	9	16	225	127	45	134	47	37%	63

Fig. 6.7 Example of Form 5

BALLOT MEASURE FORM

Precinct	Reg. Voters	Turnout	Count Yes	Count No	Turnout %	% Yes	% No	UV
1	707	552	263	202	78	48	37	
2	680	507	252	188	75	50	37	
3	705	566	305	196	80	54	35	
4	714	501	270	184	70	54	37	
5	639	473	240	189	74	51	40	
6	813	622	296	229	77	48	37	
7	696	487	216	200	70	44	41	
8	858	593	251	248	69	42	25	
9	915	606	291	218	66	48	36	
10	660	403	136	149	61	34	37	
11	752	507	226	208	67	45	41	
12	642	454	233	161	71	51	35	
13	693	531	239	242	77	45	46	
14	715	550	287	210	77	52	38	
15	633	509	277	188	80	54	37	
16	538	423	230	139	79	54	33	
17	734	575	301	218	78	52	38	
18	922	668	316	286	72	47	43	
19	728	506	240	224	70	47	44	
20	1,061	744	321	350	70	43	47	
21	150	101	44	50	67	44	50	
22	676	449	171	239	66	38	53	

Chapter 7

Canvassing

In this chapter

Map Packets

Organizing the Volunteer Force

Scheduling the Volunteers

In general, to get a vote, you must ask for a voter's vote anywhere from three to eight times. You can ask in ads in the newspaper, on TV, in direct mail, on lawn signs, or by canvassing. In small communities, canvassing is a great way to get a feel for your constituency and their concerns, and it can also be among the most elevating and gratifying experiences in a campaign.

However, canvassing is not about changing minds. It is about changing voter turnout. You can do that by going to the door of likely supporters, thereby reminding them that you need their votes to win. *Canvassing is about activating supporters—that is, getting them to vote.*

Please, do not think you will go into a neighborhood, drop off a piece of campaign literature, and have someone read it, hit herself on the forehead, and say, "My God, I have been a fool! *This* is the candidate for me." It doesn't work that way. Canvassing does not change minds. Nine out of ten people don't even read the material. Your hope is that they will place it somewhere in their houses and remember the name or ballot measure while voting. Don't get me wrong; there will be a few who thoughtfully read and digest the material and even change their minds, but they are the minority. When you canvass, you are simply *activating* people already sympathetic to your cause or candidate.

I have never worked in a campaign where I did not canvass. Canvassing is an effective and inexpensive way to get your message to the voters. It can also be a great way to get a feel for your chances of winning. In my last mayor's race the lawn signs for the opposition lined the main street through town making things look bleak. However, after I started canvassing, I realized how handily we would win, and I felt much more relaxed in all my campaign activities because of this. Canvassing will give you this information, and it will help you get additional lawn-sign locations in key spots.

If done right, you will also get valuable feedback on what the voter concerns are so that you can shape and mold advertising and debate emphasis to meet those concerns. For example, in one very controversial campaign I worked on, a woman who should have been fully behind our cause and who, in fact, had agreed to a lawn sign, told a canvasser that she was unsure about her vote because of all the controversy and the number of lawn signs for the opposition. (Note: A good canvasser will get this information back to you.) I already knew that the opposition had placed lawn signs exclusively on the main street through town. I hoped that it just *looked* worse than it was. However, with this feedback it was clear we had trouble. So with less than a week left before the election, I got together with my ad person to create a flyer in response. In our flyer we identified the opposition, as well as the money and reasons behind their opposition. Three days before the election about 90 people canvassed the city with this one-page flyer that cost next to nothing to produce. I am convinced it was the single biggest reason why we won that campaign.

Canvassing is a time-consuming, resource-intensive way to activate sympathetic voters and to bring your message to the people. Nevertheless, there are few, if any, campaign activities that will give a bigger return on investment.

With that said, it is important to note that canvassing is not for everyone. Sadly, some cities are too risky for the traditional canvass. Please be careful and know the area you are going into. Never send someone to canvass alone or go alone yourself, and never enter a house, if for no other reason than your partner will not be able to find you.

Map Packets

Before volunteers or the candidate can canvass the electorate, you must determine where to expend your efforts (through precinct analysis), and you must prepare maps of those areas for your canvassers. After these tasks have been completed, the canvassing activity itself begins. Although I always do the precinct analysis and map preparation myself, I like to break my city in half and have two canvass coordinators. If you are in a bigger city, you may

"It does not matter where we are so much as where we are heading."

Goethe

want to break it down even further. If it is a county, keep breaking it down so that people can oversee manageable units of people and space.

Setting up canvass map packets is a critical element to a successful canvass. Do not wait to do this with the canvassers when they first arrive. Map packets should be organized and ready when volunteers walk in the door. Remember the rule about not overburdening your volunteers. Set up all activities so your volunteers can see that this is an efficient, well-organized effort.

Setting up map packets for canvassing begins by going to the county clerk and getting a precinct map booklet for your county. This booklet consists of large photocopies of the county with the precincts outlined in bold and precinct numbers written on top of each of the voter precincts. If you are running a city election or a school board election, you will not need the entire book of county maps, so make copies of what you do need. Then put the county book away for future use.

Typical voter precincts have 400-500 voters, and depending on how spread-out or concentrated they are, they take six people working in pairs about two hours to complete. Larger or more difficult precincts I give to eight people for a two-hour shift. If it's your campaign, you should know your precincts better than anyone. If you don't, hop in the car and take a little drive.

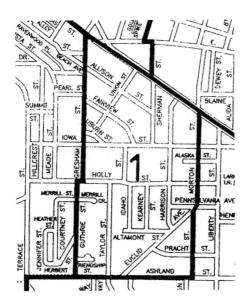

Fig. 7.1 Example of Canvassing Map

To accommodate a six-person team canvassing in pairs, you need to break precincts into thirds. If you're using eight canvassers, divide them into fourths. Precincts are often separated from one another down the middle of a street which, for canvassing purposes, is a little silly. Consider when dividing precincts for canvassing teams that you generally want one team to take both sides of a street. Also, it will sometimes be more efficient to include a section from two precincts. You know your area best. As long as the territory assigned is equal to about one-third of a precinct, things should work out fine even if you mix some precincts together.

On the canvass maps for the pairs, highlight in yellow the part of the precinct that you want the canvassers to hit. Be sure to line up your team maps on a window, or at least side by side, to check that streets haven't been missed or double-colored on different packets. Canvassing houses twice is wasteful of volunteer time and annoying to both your volunteers and the voters. It's bound to happen, but do your best to minimize it.

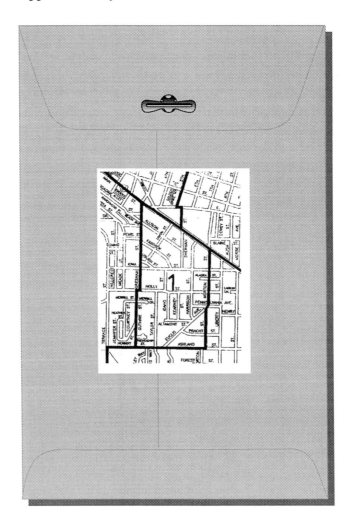

*Fig. 7.2 Example of
Canvassing Map Packet*

You will need two highlighted maps for each pair of canvassers. Everyone needs a map to work with. No exceptions. I don't care how well someone claims to know the area. Have canvassers mark off the blocks they complete on their map. This information helps you keep track of both the canvass and canvassers.

To get your canvassing teams ready to hit the streets, you will need many large manila envelopes, about six per precinct. I have one whole drawer in my office where I collect used envelopes to reuse for campaigns. If you tell your friends that you need some, you'll likely have more than you can use in a very short time or buy them at a stationary store and charge it to the campaign. You may also reuse manila envelopes during a campaign. For example, once an area has been canvassed, pull the map from the front of the envelope and tape another map in its place.

Take each of your pairs of color-coded maps and attach one map to the outside of a manila envelope. Remember, you will have two packets that are identical because people work in pairs, and these will need to stay together. Sometimes I will fold the duplicate manila envelope with the map on it and stuff it inside its partner, or I staple them together. If they get separated, you are bound to have two different teams pick up the same packet and canvass the same area two times. So pay attention to this detail.

Place the materials necessary for the type of canvass you are conducting into each envelope. If you are doing a get-out-the-vote (GOTV) or using walking lists to contact particular people, this is the packet in which you place those materials. Just put all of the lists inside one envelope and the matching envelope inside with them. The canvassers will separate out the walking lists when they divide up how they want to work. You may either place a bunch of brochures into the packet or leave them loose by the door for the volunteers to pick up on their way out. Either way, volunteers should still take additional brochures so they do not run out before they have finished their areas. Having map packets keeps brochures looking pretty fresh by the time they reach the door step, and it will also protect them in bad weather.

I often tape a 3 x 5 card on the back of the envelope. That way, if someone canvasses the home of a strong supporter, the canvasser can write it on the card and the information will get back to the campaign in a form that's easy to use. For example, supporters may tell the canvasser that they want a lawn sign or would like to be in an endorsement ad or to contribute money if the candidate calls. The canvasser can write this down on the 3x5. When a canvasser returns, just pull off the card and process it. If you do not have time to tape a 3x5 card to every canvasser's envelope, it works nearly as well to have the canvasser just write down the information directly on the envelope.

This method, however, requires that you make sure to get that information off before the envelope goes out again.

Make sure you have enough pens so each canvasser has one. I will remind people to bring pens when I call back about the canvass, but there will be those who forget. It is a nice touch to have your canvasser write on the front of the brochure "Sorry we missed you," for people not at home.

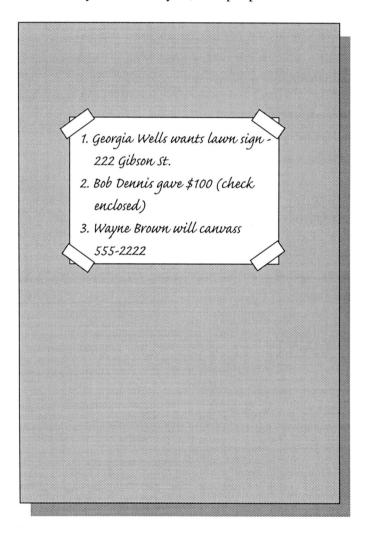

Fig. 7.3 Example of 3x5 note card attached to back side of canvass packet

Sometimes I will staple a personalized message from neighbors in a particular precinct to the brochure. If you do this, you must stuff these brochures inside the canvassing packet. Otherwise, canvassers will get confused and grab the wrong brochures. This is an inexpensive way to get a direct mail testimonial to the doors of potential supporters and well worth the effort to have it ready for the canvassers.

Consider posting a large map of your city or county on a wall where you can mark off areas as they get canvassed. Color code the wall map according to high, medium, or low canvass priority. As volunteers complete streets, mark them off in different colored inks. In this way volunteers get to see their collective work and feel part of a well run campaign.

In Summary

1. Get precinct maps from the county clerk and make plenty of photo copies of the areas you want to canvass.

2. Break each precinct down into thirds.

3. Make duplicates of each portion of the precinct and keep them together for people canvassing in pairs.

4. Yellow highlight the portion of the precinct that each pair of volunteers is to canvass and attach precinct maps to the outside of a large manila envelope.

5. Tape a 3x5 card to the manila envelope for volunteers to write notes from households offering lawn-sign locations, volunteers, or money.

6. If specialized notes are to go to specific precincts along with the brochures, place those stapled to brochures inside the manila envelope. Otherwise, have plenty of brochures available for volunteers to grab on their way out the door with their packets.

7. Provide pens or pencils inside each of the packets.

8. Have volunteers mark areas that they canvassed on the maps on their manila envelopes. Keep track of your progress on a large map on your wall by coloring in streets as they are completed.

9. Send out crews to finish up partially completed precincts as indicated on returned maps.

10. Once attached maps are completed, remove and reuse the manila envelopes.

Note: I make duplicates of all my highlighted maps. That way I have a complete set to prepare map packets for future campaigns. Don't give in and use your originals when you're in a hurry, or you'll be sorry the next time you need them.

"Life has taught me we must put our convictions into action."
Margaret Sanger

Organizing the Volunteer Force

Have your volunteers arrive 15 minutes early if they have not canvassed for you before. The moment they walk in, ask them to read the brochure to familiarize themselves with the contents. Generally, I have out a plate of cookies or brownies or some little something to eat, plus juice and water. I have coffee on hand if someone asks for it, but I do not set it out as people will have to go to the bathroom the minute they get out the door (and generally they will go back home to do that.) Coffee or not, urge people to use the bathroom *before* they head out to canvass.

In training canvassers, I tell them never to talk the issues. That is for the candidate or the campaign team. No canvasser, I don't care how closely related, can possibly know how a candidate stands on all the issues. So what do canvassers say when asked a question at the door? They can say, "That is a good question. Why don't you give Elle a call and ask her." Never offer to have the candidate call to answer a question. He or she will get little else done, and a voter who truly wants to know will take a moment to pick up the phone.

			Activity: Canvassing (City & Date)	
NAME	PHONE #	CB?	9:30 AM–12:00	2:30–5:00

Fig. 7.4 Example of 5x8 Canvassing Activity Card

The only thing canvassers can truthfully say is why *they* are out working for the candidate. It might be because of the candidate's stand on the environment, development, timber, air quality, transportation, children's issues, taxes, jobs, or human resources. Every person who works for you will have a reason for volunteering. Urge your volunteers to think what that reason is before they head out to walk. This directive should be part of your pre-canvassing spiel. Be sure to include things like: "What would motivate you to get out and canvass on a beautiful Saturday when you would probably rather be home with your families?" This is also a nice way to let volunteers know you understand what they are giving up to work for you and that you appreciate it. I also include in my pep talks or training how difficult the odds are of winning the campaign, and how important it is that we, not the opposition, win. This brings out the best in your workers.

Scheduling the Volunteers

More than anywhere else in the campaign, I try to accommodate volunteers' schedules for canvassing. Generally I set up four time slots for people on a given weekend. However, if none of those times works for individuals, I will send them out when they can go. Nine times out of ten there will be someone else who can or has to go at that time, so I can provide a partner. If I can't get a partner for the individual, I usually go along myself. I do this because it is safer and it is good for the candidate or campaign manager to canvass. In this way you become more empathic to the efforts of your canvassers, get a better understanding of the voters, and demonstrate your willingness to work as hard as the volunteers. Volunteers love to canvass with the candidate or campaign manager.

I think it is also important to do special things for your canvassers. If someone tells me she does not like to do hills or that she wants to do her neighborhood, I make sure to set that packet aside for her and tell her that I will be setting aside her request. This further eliminates potential no-shows.

A big part of a good canvassing effort is placing the right volunteer in the right precinct. For example, if you have an area with a senior population, place your oldest canvassers in that area. If you have canvassers whose dress is odd or in some way inappropriate, put them in a more progressive area or have them work lawn signs. Peers should canvass peers. Whomever you assign, remember that when they knock at the door, they represent the campaign. I generally let people know before they canvass that they must present themselves well to the public and look nice.

"The first thing you naturally do is teach the person to feel that the undertaking is manifestly important and nearly impossible. . . . That draws out the kind of drives that make people strong."
Edwin H. Land, Founder, Polaroid Corp.

Sometimes you will have volunteers in areas of swing voters, and many times these swing voters are overwhelmingly registered with one party over another. (Remember swing voters are people who do not always vote party lines but rather tend to vote issues.) I will try to place a canvasser who is the same party affiliation as the precinct. For example, if I am working for a Democrat and need to canvass a neighborhood that is predominantly Republican, I get my Republican volunteers together and have them canvass the neighborhood. That way when someone answers the door and says they vote party line, the canvasser can say: "I know, I'm a Republican and I usually do too, but this election I'm working for a Democrat because. . . ."

Bad Weather

There are bound to be days of bad weather scheduled for canvassing. When I am working on a campaign, I pray for a rainy drizzle. And I tell my canvassers to pray for rain and dress accordingly. Why? Because, when it rains, more people are home and your campaign gets bonus points for getting out in bad weather. People open the door and feel sorry for you and admire your dedication. I have also noticed that volunteers don't mind canvassing in bad weather. Think about it. If it is a sunny glorious spring or fall day, wouldn't you rather be out doing something other than canvassing? If the weather is lousy, canvassing is a good thing to do with your time.

Although volunteer recruitment has already been covered in depth, one very effective technique I have found for getting more people to canvass is to ask every person who has agreed to canvass to bring a friend. This makes it more fun for that individual, increases your volunteer numbers, and helps to reduce possible no-shows. Since canvassing is conducted in pairs, it is an ideal activity for friends or couples. It is also safer in two's.

Remember, put no campaign literature in or on mail boxes and also be sure your campaign material does not become litter. When residents are not home, instruct volunteers to wedge it into door jambs, screen doors, and trim boards so that it cannot escape into the wind.

If you are the candidate, it is fine to use volunteers to help with the canvassing. However, because it is much more effective for the candidate to knock on the door, the candidate must cover as much ground as possible. Don't, however, overdo it. Pace yourself. Start early enough in the campaign so that you canvass as many homes as possible. The personal touch really works. The candidate should have someone to work with, if possible. It's also helpful to have someone else covering the area because the candidate is likely to get hung up talking with the voters.

In Summary

It bears repeating that it is critical to a successful campaign to have a large number of people turn out to volunteer. Canvassers feel good when they are clearly part of a larger effort. They are further reinforced in their commitment to the campaign when they show up and see friends and neighbors there working as well.

1. Carefully select your canvassing volunteers. Use people who are in relatively good shape and individuals who are able to walk for two hours at a time. Save apartments or areas of flat, heavy concentration for individuals who are out of shape.

2. Select the right volunteer for the right precinct. Peers should canvass peers. Have volunteers canvass their neighborhoods.

3. Accommodate the schedule of the canvassers. If they cannot make the scheduled time, find a time when they can and find them a partner. This is a great way to finish up partially completed precincts.

4. Use the same 5" x 8" cards to sign up volunteers for the canvass.

5. Call back (CB?) your volunteers to make sure they will still be coming. Remember, do not ask if they still intend to canvass. Instead, remind them to bring something or ask what time you told them to come in case you made a mistake.

6. On the call back, reschedule volunteers who forgot about the canvass.

7. Ask volunteers to bring a friend.

8. First thing, have your canvassers read what they will be dropping at homes. They should be familiar with the material.

9. Set up a role-play door-knocking demonstration as part of the volunteer training before volunteers head out the door.

10. Do not serve coffee or tea to canvassers before they head out, only juice or water. Remind them to use the bathroom before they leave.

11. Remind your workers of the law: no brochures in or on mailboxes. Remind them also to secure materials left at doorsteps to prevent litter.

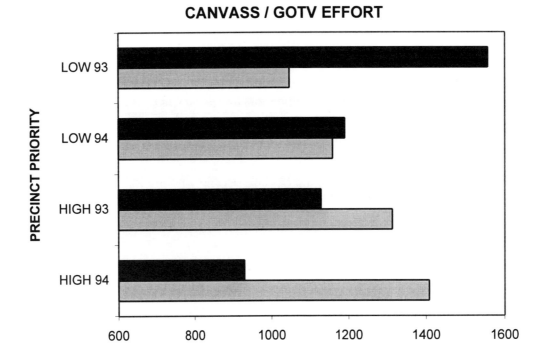

CANVASS / GOTV EFFORT

Fig. 7.5 A case for canvassing and GOTV

A dramatic example of the effectiveness of combining canvassing and getting out the vote (outlined in the next chapter) is provided in Figure 7.5. Identical ballot measures were placed before Ashland voters in 1993 and then a year later in 1994. Our supporting campaigns were exactly the same with two exceptions: first, in 1993 both high and low priority precincts were canvassed, whereas in 1994, only high priority precincts were. Second, only in 1994 did we make a voter ID and GOTV effort. The combination of activating only high support precincts with a GOTV worked. The same measure that lost in 1993 by 326 votes passed in 1994 by 447 votes.

In Figure 7.5, note the decrease of "no" votes in the low priority precincts between the two elections. Because these precincts were not canvassed in 1994, fewer voters were activated to get out and vote. The increase in the "yes" votes for the low priority precincts in 1994 over 1993 is a result of the voter ID and GOTV effort.

Because the 1993 election was a "mail-in," it had an overall higher voter turnout than the walk-in 1994 election. Mail-in elections always have a higher voter turnout.

Chapter 8

Getting Out the Vote (GOTV)

In this chapter

Identifying Your Voters: Voter ID

Canvassing for Voter ID

Voter ID by Phone

Poll Watching

Phoning

The Absentee Ballot

Mail-in Elections

If canvassing is about activating people who you *think* will vote for your cause, then a GOTV effort is about activating voters who you *know* will vote for your cause. Finding out how they intend to vote is called Voter ID. Getting them out to vote on *election day* is called getting out the vote or GOTV.

GOTV is also different from canvassing in that you are not just going to specific precincts but rather to specific voters. Obviously this means you need to identify how the voter intends to vote. This can be done in one of two ways:

1. You can ask every household you canvass how they will vote and mark it on walking lists. These lists can be bought from a voter ID service, such as voter contact services.

2. Or, you can call people in favorable precincts that are inclined to vote for your candidate and simply ask. You can buy a list of registered voters by precinct from the county.

"Persistence in the face of adversity is what wins an election."
Patricia Schifferle
Pacific Advocates

A GOTV effort is most effective in elections where there is great voter apathy and an anticipated low voter turnout. Your mission is to increase the voter turnout of *certain* segments of the population only—that is, those voting the way you want them to vote. Getting out the vote means getting these people to the polls or getting them to return their mail-in ballots.

If you are involved in an elective office election where a controversial measure is also on the ballot, there may be a high voter turnout. If the controversial measure is one that the supporters of your candidate tend to favor, your supporters will very likely be voting, no matter what you do. This kind of thing tends to limit the effectiveness of a GOTV effort. However, there is nothing as important to winning a close campaign as a good GOTV.

Identifying Your Voters: Voter ID

Before you can get out the vote, you need to identify voters who will be supporting your candidate or measure. One way to get the information you need is to get printed voter walking lists from a voter contact service firm. In my state we have a firm that can put together just about any combination you could think of. To find one in your state, try contacting elected officials, campaign firms, or call 1-800-995-5859.

Note: if you are working on a local election where no similar election was held at a statewide level, you must first conduct a precinct analysis. You then tell the voter contact service which precincts you want walking lists for.

Explain to the voter contact service that you want to use these lists to identify voters for a GOTV effort. They will list potential supporters based on past *precinct* voting trends and list them according to precinct by street address and in numerical order. The voters on each street will be listed on a separate page. Across the top of the page will read: "supporting," "leaning support," "undecided," "leaning no support," and "not supporting" (or a number rating system correlated with these categories). Next to each registered voter's name will be a number from one to five that corresponds to the categories from "supporting" to "not supporting."

As indicated before, you may also get walking lists of identified priority precincts from the county. If you do this, *you* must do the precinct analysis first (see Chapter 6: "Precinct Analysis") and tell the county which precincts you want. Once you have the walking lists, there are two ways you can voter ID: one is by canvassing, and the other is by phone.

Canvassing for Voter ID

If you intend to do voter ID while canvassing, you need to reorganize the contact service's walking lists to coincide with your canvassing maps. Your canvassers must have the contact list that goes with the canvassing area they are assigned to. This is a lot more work than you might imagine. *Do not let just anyone help you with this task!!!* or you'll spend days undoing and redoing. Once you match a walking list to a canvassing map, place the list *inside* the canvassing envelope.

If you are canvassing for a GOTV effort, you will need twice the number of canvassers normally required *or more*. At the door, each of your canvassers must ascertain whether the house will be in favor, opposed, undecided, or leaning in some way. If voters are leaning support or undecided, you should be ready to follow up with literature or a phone call to bring them into your camp. If no one is home, you must have clean-up teams going out to re-knock or do the voter ID at phone banks by calling to determine how people intend to vote.

The idea here is to identify individual voters who you are sure will vote for your cause if they vote. You use the results of your voter ID to compile lists of those who will vote for you, your candidate, or your cause. List your "yes" voters according to city and precinct. You must include a phone number. If some of these names come without phone numbers, set up a clerical team to look them up before election day.

If this sounds like a lot of work, it is. If you are going to do a GOTV effort, you will need someone to watch over it specifically. And everyone who has volunteered at some time during the campaign must work on election night. Actually, getting volunteers to work election night is a surprisingly easy thing to do. People who work on a campaign often have excess energy on campaign night and love to be part of the final big push.

Although it puts a big burden on the phone bank team, I tend to prefer voter ID by phone for a number of reasons:

1. Some canvassed areas have only 40% of the households with anyone at home during the canvass. That means that the remaining homes have to be called or recanvassed.

2. It is generally easier to get phone volunteers than canvass volunteers, and canvassing for ID eats up people.

3. I believe people will tend to be more honest on the phone. It is hard for individuals to tell candidates or volunteers face-to-face that

they will be supporting the opposition, especially if they made all that effort to come to the person's door step.

Coordinating all these people is a job-and-a-half, so be prepared.

Voter ID by Phone

Conducting voter ID by phone works anywhere, but it is most effective in smaller areas where you can realistically call 80% or more of the voters. Although I have seen it work effectively in large county-wide elections, it requires a huge effort. However, it is well worth it.

From a voter ID service or from the county (much cheaper), get a list of voters by precinct in alphabetical order. It is the best use of time to call only high- and medium-support precincts. To identify your supporters, you need to set up phone banks and systematically call every registered voter in the designated area. Often, county lists do not have all of the phone numbers listed, so you may need to set up clerical sessions to look up phone numbers before your phone banks begin. Phone banking to identify supporters, if you can do it, goes much quicker than canvassing. Once you have identified your supporters, there are two ways to find out if they have voted. One is poll watching and the other, much simpler method, is by phoning.

Poll Watching

On election day (for a walk-in vote, not mail-in) have teams of poll watchers at the polls noting which of your supporters have voted. It is important here to check with the county clerk to see what is legal. Poll watchers may review the poll book as long as they do not interfere with the work of the election board and they do not remove the poll book from the election board table.

In high-priority precincts, have poll watchers keeping track of who among your identified supporters has voted and who has not. As the name of the voter is called out, the poll watcher will check the list of supporters to see whether that individual is among those who have been positively identified. This information is relayed back to phone banks, and approximately four hours before the polls close, supporters who have not yet voted get a call from a volunteer urging them to get down to the polls. Regardless of what you think about the outcome of the election, tell the volunteers to impress upon the voters how important it is that they get to the polls, that you predict a very close election, and that every vote will count. The supporter who hasn't yet voted must have a sense of urgency to get to the polls and vote.

Rides are offered to get supporters to and from the polls. If there is a sleeping baby or child, a volunteer may offer to come stay in the home while the single parent votes. Among the poll watcher, the phone bank, and the transportation effort, you will have a lot of people involved. Only a well-organized, well-run campaign can pull off an effective GOTV. That is one reason well-organized and well-run campaigns win elections.

Poll watching is a great activity to do with another campaign. Two candidates or a candidate and measure with similar support bases can coordinate their volunteer forces for the poll-watching effort.

Phoning

Let's suppose that you do not have enough people to watch the polling places all day. Don't worry. I recently worked on a campaign where we came up with an approach that was nearly as effective and won handily because of the GOTV effort. For this process you will need a good precinct analysis. Remember, your precinct analysis will tell you where your support is. It will show you where people have voted for causes similar to yours in the past. Your precinct analysis will also tell you where people live who will *never* vote for your cause or candidate. If it is clear that a precinct has traditionally voted against campaigns such as the one you are working on, don't canvass them, don't call them, don't activate them. Forget them for the GOTV effort. Instead, look for precincts that have been split: those that have narrowly supported or narrowly defeated past campaigns similar to yours. These are the precincts you should call and voter ID. Then on election day call only the *identified "yes"* voters.

As for those remaining precincts that have overwhelmingly supported past campaigns similar to the one you are now promoting, it is not so necessary to voter ID them. You know they will vote your way.

On election day, while your people are going down the list of supporters in the marginal precincts calling the *identified* "yes" votes, they can call *all* of the voters in the high priority precincts. Should your campaign have time before election day, you may want to ID the voters in the high priority precincts as well, but this is not as important. Look at the phone calling on the day of the election as your one last canvass in a high priority precinct. Call everyone. If your precinct analysis is accurate, you will turn out strong support that might have stayed home otherwise. *Remember, you are not changing minds, just the turnout.* Minds are generally made up.

One important caveat: *don't duplicate calling lists.* Each phone banker or phone station needs a separate calling list. When the caller reaches someone who has already voted, he or she needs to cross off the name so the person is not called again. For those who have not voted, it is up to you to decide whether you want to call them again. If the election is close, you may want to urge them one more time to get down to the polls. However, in general, more than one call is an annoyance and counterproductive.

The Absentee Ballot

Voting absentee used to be a service to the voter who was temporarily out of the area or unable to get to the polls. However, it has now become the vote of convenience. As ballots become longer and more complex, the busy and conscientious voter is choosing to vote absentee. In a recent California election it took my parents more than an hour to vote their twelve-card ballot. And they *knew* how they intended to vote on each of the issues. Is it any wonder they would choose to do it at home?

The absentee ballot has traditionally been a more conservative vote, but it has gotten even more so simply because only campaigns with enormous resources are capable of capitalizing on the absentee voter with direct mail and personalized phone calls. Absentee ballots present some unique challenges to the grassroots campaign. Here is an inexpensive way to deal with absentee ballots.

Assign the task of the absentee ballot to a team. One person must be willing to go the county clerk's office and find out who has requested absentee ballots. This person keeps a running list. This should be done on a regular basis because voters requesting the absentee ballot will fill it out and return it. Once you know who the people are making the request, you must try to persuade them to vote for your candidate or cause. Forget the precinct analysis for the absentee voter. You are no longer hoping these people will *not* be voting. You know for a fact they will. You have a number of choices.

1. Use direct mail to persuade.

2. Send volunteers or the candidate to their homes to canvass the voters.

3. Have the candidate, a friend, or prominent citizen call.

4. Send a personalized letter from the candidate or from a well known, respected local leader of the same party affiliation as the voter.

5. Use some combination of all these techniques.

Mail-in Elections

Mail-in elections have been in use in Oregon for nearly a decade now, and I think they're great. I also believe, because of budget cuts in government, they will soon be how we all vote. Although Oregon is the only state conducting mail-in elections as of this writing, in a way every state does through the absentee ballot option. For state and county government to provide the option of both absentee and poll voting with tax dollars is a costly luxury we will soon relinquish everywhere. In a recent senatorial primary, the state saved an estimated $1.7 million by having a mail-in election, rather than the more traditional walk-in election.

Mail-in elections are those where the county mails all ballots to the homes of registered voters within a specific voting district. In order to give voters ample time to review the ballot items, ballots are mailed about three weeks prior to the final election date when they must be at the county clerk's office for tabulation. The cost savings to county and state government is about 50% with the added bonus of increasing voter turnout anywhere from 10% to 30%. Higher turnout and huge savings to the taxpayer are pretty strong endorsements.

For the purposes of your campaign team, the difference for a mail-in as opposed to poll voting lies primarily in the timing of your election. In a normal election most of your canvassing and nearly all of your ads occur in the final three weeks prior to when ballots are cast. With a mail-in election, more than 50% of all the voters who return their ballots will do so in the first week after receiving the ballots. That means if you wait to do your canvass and to place your really great ads in the final three weeks, you will be doing so after the election is essentially over.

Depending on when you can place lawn signs, you might even choose to eliminate them from your campaign plan. After all, if you are restricted to placing signs 30 days before an election and voters return their mailed ballots in the first week after receiving them, is it worth the money and effort? Since many believe the impact of lawn signs comes on the first week, lawn signs will still probably do the job they are intended to do. However, this is a discussion that should take place among your campaign committee.

In general, if you are involved in a mail-in election, your campaign must peak the day the ballots are mailed, not the day they are due back. Your canvassing must be completed the day the ballots are mailed, and your ads must start and peak prior to the time ballots leave the county clerk's office. Even though most voters will return their ballots immediately, your campaign and cause should continue to have a presence in the media until the day the ballots are due. You must be prepared to spend more money on ads.

GOTV and Voter ID

After the ballots are mailed, your campaign's primary focus must turn to the get-out-the-vote effort. A GOTV effort for a mail-in election is remarkably easy and painless. It is also the best thing about mail-in elections. With a mail-in you do not need to voter ID by either canvassing or phone banks as described earlier in this chapter. The voter ID and GOTV take place in the same call. Here is how it works:

Counties keep track of who votes, and for a nominal charge ($20 or so) they will print a list of those who have voted *(activity list),* or those who haven't voted *(inactivity list).* To do a GOTV, you want to know who has *not* voted in that first week or so. Some counties do not have the capability of separating the active and inactive lists. If this is the case, consider setting up a clerical team to prepare lists for your GOTV effort.

When vote by mail was first introduced in Oregon, nearly all (80%) of all the voters who intended to vote did so within the first week. These percentages have now leveled off to 60% the first week, followed by 10% in the second week, and 30% in the final week. If you are involved in a vote-by-mail campaign, call your county clerk to determine the habits of your constituency in previous elections. You need to know the percent of people who return ballots in the first week. Then plug this number into the formula outlined in this section.

Predicting Turnout

Usually counties will run a couple of days behind, so about ten days after the ballots are mailed, call up and ask for the number of ballots already returned. The number they give you will be anywhere from 50% to 80% of the total turnout for the election. Call your county clerk for voter tendencies in your area. From this, you can figure out what the actual turnout will eventually be.

In past elections, I have used this information to help me calculate how many more ballots I need to win. For example, if you are working on a school election that in the past lost by a 45%–55% margin, with simple math you can calculate how many people will ultimately vote. Multiply that by 55%, and subtract that from the total voter turnout. The difference is what you predict you will lose by, and it also gives you the number of ballots that *must* come in during your GOTV effort to pull off a win.

Let's do it together:

Let's say you live in a city with 6000 registered voters where 60% of all of those who will return their ballots do so in the first week. Ten days after the ballots are mailed, you call and find that 2400 have returned their ballots.

We know that 2400 = 60% of total number of ballots that will eventually come in.

So we set up the following equation: 60/100 times X = 2400. (You put 60 over 100 because it is 60%.) Now you have to isolate the "x," so multiply both sides by 100 and then divide both sides by 60. X (total number of votes) = 4000 ballots that will eventually come in or a 66% voter turnout.

In the past, school elections for money have failed in your city by 55%, so multiply 55% times 4000, which equals 2200. This represents the number who will be voting against the school tax measure if you do nothing. Subtract 2200 from 4000, which equals 1800. This is the number who will be voting for your school measure. Subtract one from the other (1800 from 2200), and this tells you that if you do nothing you will lose the election by 400 votes.

Now you can go to work. You will need to order the inactivity list from the county clerk. If your county does not separate those who have voted from those who have not, line up a clerical team to highlight which ones need volunteer attention. Ask that this list be organized by precinct and that it be listed alphabetically. Although some of the county lists contain phone numbers, they are rarely complete, so you might want to set up a clerical team to look up phone numbers as well.

Distribute the high-support precincts (you determined these when you did your precinct analysis) to volunteers who are willing to call. Next, make your phone calls to convince voters leaning toward your position to support your issue. Second, you need to remind those who are supporting your effort to return their ballots.

Last-ditch Effort

All volunteers are assigned to go over copies of the list and call any friends they find. The hope is that, if friends call friends, they can move them to get their ballots in or influence the votes of the undecided. If you are out of time or energy in your campaign, you can skip this first step and simply wait for a last-ditch effort right before election day.

In one campaign when we did this, I called a friend to get her ballot in and found out that she was a "no" vote. While I could not convince her to vote "yes," I did convince her to not return her ballot.

Your last-ditch mail election GOTV should begin on the Friday preceding election day. You will need to get one last inactivity list. Again, names should be organized alphabetically according to precinct. That weekend, two to three days before the election, when it is too late to return a ballot through the mail, set up your phone banks. Your job is to call *everyone* on that list whether supporting your measure or not. Start with high-priority precincts where you will be most successful and then work your way through the rest as ballots are needed.

When you contact someone, you must first determine if she or he is supportive. If so, say that someone is on the way over to pick up the ballot. If the person is not supporting, get off the phone. Don't worry about activating "no" votes. The chances of a nonsupporting person driving to the county offices who hasn't already mailed in the ballot is minuscule. Collect ballots all weekend, and on Monday or Tuesday morning have campaign workers deliver all the ballots to the county. In a close mail-in election, those votes will win you the campaign.

Chapter 9

Direct Mail

In this chapter

Direct Mail to Hit Your Opponent

Direct Mail on a Budget

Mail Preparation

Whereas canvassing is about activating voters who are inclined to vote for your candidate according to the past voting patterns of their neighborhood, direct mail is about activating voters around a specific issue that transcends voting tendencies. As discussed in the section on brochures, the first thing you do with your campaign committee is to develop a message or theme for the campaign. Through the process of identifying why and who will vote for your cause, you identify groups with which your candidate or campaign will develop a relationship. This process and message are developed early to activate special interest support that can lead to endorsements, money, and, yes, votes.

Direct mail cultivates a relationship between your campaign and the voters, based on issues. The purpose is to swing their votes your way— regardless of party affiliation or prior voting tendencies.

For example, you are working for a pro-choice Republican running against an anti-choice Democrat. You have a list of pro-choice voters who tend to vote party. Your job is to point out that their Democrat is anti-choice. You're banking on their ideals swinging their votes. Believe me, it works. The strategy you use here is an issue-based campaign. With these voters you stay on this message.

It works because you are offering the voters simple, additional information to help them decide an issue or candidate. Direct mail is a way to get a specialized message to individual voters regardless of where they live or how their precincts tend to vote. You can run your entire issue-based campaign on direct mail; all it takes is money. However, in a grassroots campaign where resources are limited and jurisdictions somewhat smaller, direct mail can best be used to augment the more comprehensive, less expensive campaign.

Direct mail is more than a letter or brochure stuffed into an envelope. It is the most selective of all media forms, and, because of its selectivity, there are distinct advantages of using direct mail over TV, newspapers, or radio. Using direct mail, a campaign can align an exact issue with an exact voter in a specific house. To do this effectively requires research on the part of the campaign, as you must know your opponent's stands on specific issues and you also must know the issues that will swing a particular voter. Ideally you will find areas that matter to the voter in which your candidate and the opponent differ dramatically from one another. *These are called "ticket splitters." A ticket splitter is an issue that is so important to the voter that it, and it alone, will drive how a vote is cast.* In general, ticket splitters are emotional votes and do not track party lines.

It is important to remember that your *direct mail* is *only as effective as the list to which it is mailed.*

Let me give you some areas that separate out voters motivated by issue.

Military Votes: For example, you are running against an incumbent who was one of two "no" votes in the state senate on a bill designed to protect job security of National Guard volunteers after a military rotation. This is information that the Vets should have.

Libraries: Your opponent voted to close the public library during tight budget years while voting to increase his salary. Friends of the Library, district school teachers, volunteers associated with the libraries, and faculty and students at a local college should know this.

Woman's Right to Choose: Your school board opponent voted against sexuality education in the high school curriculum, and teen pregnancy increased threefold. Supporters of NARAL, Women's Political Caucus, American Association of University Women, Planned Parenthood, and the Presbyterian and Unitarian Churches should know this.

Environmental Issues (*timber, rivers, desert, parks, wildlife areas*): Again, environmentalist or anti-environmentalists issues do not track party lines. Stands in these areas should be delivered to a specific voting constituency.

Other ticket splitters:
- *Air quality*
- *Traffic (congestion, bikes, pedestrian walkways, mass transit)*
- *Airports, especially general aviation*
- *Seniors*
- *Schools, teachers, children issues*
- *Unions*
- *Children's athletic programs*
- *Small businesses*
- *Land use, development and parks*
- *Taxes*
- *Other issues specific to your community*

Direct mail has about a three-second life. You must first get the receiver to open it, and then there must be something there to grab the person.

One great piece of direct mail I saw had two well-known people who had been in opposing camps on a number of issues, standing back to back, arms crossed, looking at the camera. The caption was something to the effect that "Bob and Sam can agree only on one thing." Following was the campaign issue they both agreed upon with a vote "yes" at the bottom.

Here are some tips to make your direct mail more effective:

1. Have no paragraphs with more than three sentences.

2. Have no sentences with more than ten words.

3. Ninety-five percent of the words should be two syllables or fewer.

4. If it is a letter, personalize wherever possible: in the salutation and signature, a handwritten or typed "P.S.," and especially a hand-addressed envelope (use a clerical team).

5. Look crisp. The direct mail reflects on the candidate's taste and organization. If the piece looks shoddy, it tells prospective voters that the candidate thinks they aren't worth anything better.

6. Get a professional to organize "a look" and allow enough money for high-quality production. Consider direct mail that doesn't go in an envelope.

7. Plan your direct mail: make it coincide with a relevant news item or legislative action that will reinforce your campaign message. For example, you are running against an anti-choice state representative. A vote comes before the legislative assembly on parental notification for minors prior to having an abortion, and you know your opponent

"Follow the money."
Patricia Schifferle,
Pacific Advocates

will vote "yes." Have a hit piece ready for your pro-choice voters with this information and more.

8. Decide in advance what your direct mail will say, how it will look, to whom it will be sent, and when it will be sent.

Direct Mail to Hit Your Opponent

I do not consider pointing out how my opponent has voted as negative campaigning. While I try to avoid it in debates and ads, in the privacy of the voter's home I will point out the past voting record of my opponent or how the opposition has lied in their campaign materials.

In order to hit your opponent or the opposition effectively with direct mail, you must do your homework. Know from where the money for the opposing campaign is coming. Know past voting records, if it is a candidate, and, as with issues, follow the money and follow the endorsements. Look at the principles on which the opposition is basing its campaign—that is, their campaign message. If their voting record directly opposes their message, it speaks to integrity. Campaign themes, such as voting records, are fair game. For example, if the brochure for the opposition has pictures of children and speaks of strong school support, yet the voting record of the candidate shows no school support.

When at all possible, hit your opposition in a clever way or with humor. One of the best direct mail opponent hits I have seen using humor came out of New Jersey. New Jersey has unbelievably high auto insurance premiums. An assemblywoman ran for her first election campaign on a platform of going after auto insurance rates. However, once elected, the only legislation she introduced was for pet insurance. In the next election, her opponent used direct mail to deliver a full glossy close-up of a trimmed and fluffed poodle, wearing diamond shaped sunglasses and bow in its hair, sitting behind the steering wheel of a very nice red convertible. The caption below the dog read, "She promised to fix our insurance problem . . . ." On the inside of the brochure was a close-up of just the dog looking straight at the camera with the text that said, "Unfortunately [name] is fixing the wrong one." The picture was surrounded by text elaborating on this woman's voting record and ineffectiveness in office.

Another clever ad had a cutout of the busts of James Madison, George Washington, and Thomas Jefferson on card stock. Directly below their busts were their signatures and below those a single question: "Who wrote the Declaration of Independence?" You flip it over and it says, "[Name of candidate] doesn't care if our kids never know." It goes on to explain how this candidate voted against a measure brought to the state legislature by parents making the Declaration of Independence, the Constitution, and the Federalist Papers required reading.

A voting record is not only a verifiable fact, but a fact that goes to the very essence of why we have elections. In a county-wide campaign, I usually have one volunteer researching voting records. This can bring interesting information together for the campaign to use in direct mailing or for the candidate to use in debates.

Direct mail is different from targeting neighborhoods for canvassing in precinct analysis but similar in that you are directing your pitch for voter *interest* areas rather than simple voting proclivity patterns. Also keep in mind that, by using direct mail, you can address subjects that, if put in the paper, might activate a lot of nasty letters-to-the-editor. Well targeted direct mail reaches potential friends of the campaign and lets them know where you (or your opponent) stand and where to send money. Used properly, direct mail is very effective.

Direct Mail on a Budget

Most campaigns are, of course, short on money. If that is the case, consider combining direct mail with canvassing. I recently worked on a campaign where we walked direct mail stuffed in the brochures to neighborhoods. In this particular campaign, we were trying to fund an open space/ parks program. Each neighborhood of the city was slated for a park in the plan. So we drafted a specialized campaign piece pointing out what kind of park each specific neighborhood would get. We then asked four to six supporters from that neighborhood to sign their names under the piece, and volunteers walked it into the appropriate neighborhood as part of our canvassing effort. In this way the campaign piece became both a personal letter and endorsement. We also had neighbors canvassing neighbors. The technique was extremely effective and was certainly a contributing factor in our city's becoming the first in Oregon to pass a food and beverage sales tax in order to fund a parks program. This program won state recognition in "Cities Awards for Excellence Program."

Walking in direct mail becomes more difficult (if not dangerous) when you are dealing with hot-button issues such as choice or land use. This is where your precinct analysis will help. However, in most small towns and counties, specific issues will be important in certain neighborhoods. If you can connect the issues with the neighborhoods, walking direct mail can be very effective and far cheaper than mailing it, or printing up three or four different campaign brochures.

Walking direct mail to the door is also a good way to time your mailing. In one campaign I worked on, we walked a "hit" direct mail piece three days before the election. In the piece we pointed out nothing more than who was financing the other side. It worked for two reasons. First, it obviously showed that our side was rich with volunteers and not money, as close to 100 people walked the streets for that canvass. And second, because of the timing, the opposition did not have time to respond before election day.

Mail Preparation

Once you have decided what you are going to do and the direct mail piece has been written, printed, and is back at your home in boxes, you must complete the following:

1. Organize a clerical work team to assemble your direct mail. If there is a letter or brochure, that needs to get stuffed into an envelope along with other enclosures. If you are mailing out a simple information piece, you can cut costs and work by printing your message on one side of a single sheet of paper. Have your clerical team come in and fold the piece in half, stamp it, address it, and if needed, place a return address on it. You do not need to staple. Using a bright color here can increase the likelihood that someone will look at it. Keep the message simple. You may also choose to do mass invitations to a fund-raiser on card stock using half sheets of 8 1/2 x 11 and send them as oversized postcards. However, if it is a nice fund-raiser, you may well want it in an envelope looking the part. Whatever the task for your clerical work team, have it all lined up and ready to go.

2. Once the mailing is stuffed or folded (if it is a single page with no envelope), you must address it. Hand addressing and stick-on stamps really increase the number of people who will open and look inside. However, if you are mailing to specific precincts, you may prefer to hire a voter contact service to print labels.

3. As pieces get addressed, they must be kept separate according to zip codes. Once things are bundled according to zip codes, take the bundles to the post office and ask for help on how many they want in each bundle, which post office stickers go on which, and what forms to fill out. If lingering at the post office is a hassle, bundle all mail with the same five-digit zip code, in groups of ten or more per pack, with rubber bands. Packs should be no greater than two inches thick. The rubber bands go horizontally and vertically. For groups of less than ten with the same zip, bundle those with other envelopes matching the first three zip numbers. For example: 975̲20, 975̲23, 975̲40, 975̲01. You must

know the count of your entire mailing. Make sure that each component of the mailing is exactly the same. For example, I once did a mailing with a #6 remittance envelope stuffed inside. However, I ran out of the #6 envelopes and stuffed a slightly larger one I had in stock. You can't do this. Each component of each piece must weigh the same.

Take your bundles to the post office to fill out the paper work and place appropriate post office stickers on the front of each bundle. They will provide stickers and forms.

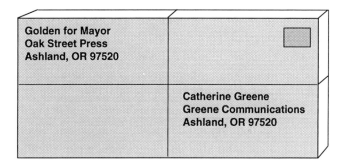

Fig. 9.1 Example of Direct Mail Package

4. Direct mail may be hired out rather than using volunteers. Take your camera-ready art plus your mailing list printed in a specific format for labels (call ahead to get the specifics) to a mailing house, and they will take care of everything else, including getting it to the post office.

5. Be aware that some colors of ink will not work for post office scanners Check these things out ahead of time.

Chapter 10

Media

In this chapter

Timing Your Ads

Advertising Formats

Endorsements and Endorsement Ads

Letters-to-the-Editor and Free Media

Other Free Media Coverage

Getting on the Front Page and Creating Media Events

Fielding Questions from the Press

Radio and Television

Bumper Stickers and Buttons

The media has a way of legitimizing your cause or your candidate. People are always saying, "It must be true; I read it in the paper" or "They wouldn't print it if it wasn't true." Don't waste the legitimizing effect of the media. Promote yourself and your ideas in a believable way rather than tearing down your opponent, and you'll get the most from your media budget.

Your campaign theme and message must be at the center of your media efforts. Although there will be times when you must answer attacks, do so and then get back on your message as quickly as possible. Use each question to bring the topic around to your message. As I indicated before, once you lay out your campaign, assess your strengths and weaknesses, and establish your message, the media will be your best avenue for bringing this message to the voter. If you take too long in establishing who you are, the opposition will define you first, and the rest of the campaign will be spent digging your way out of a hole.

While I dislike negative campaigning, it is inherent in the process. After all you are running because you embrace values different from your opponent's. If you are working for or against a measure, there is a reason, and as you define that reason, you not only define who you are but who your opposition is. The inverse is true also. If your opponent is telling the voters what he or she represents as opposed to you, your opponent is defining you or your campaign. If nothing comes from your side, that definition gains credibility.

Establish your campaign theme early and stick to it. Raise your money early, and schedule your media buys early.

In this chapter I have included examples of ads. In general, I use three ad formats when I am working on a campaign: emotional ads, information ads, and endorsement ads. Sometimes I will mix up the style of my ads, for example, an endorsement ad with pictures that elicit an emotion. Ad styles can be combined. They are not mutually exclusive.

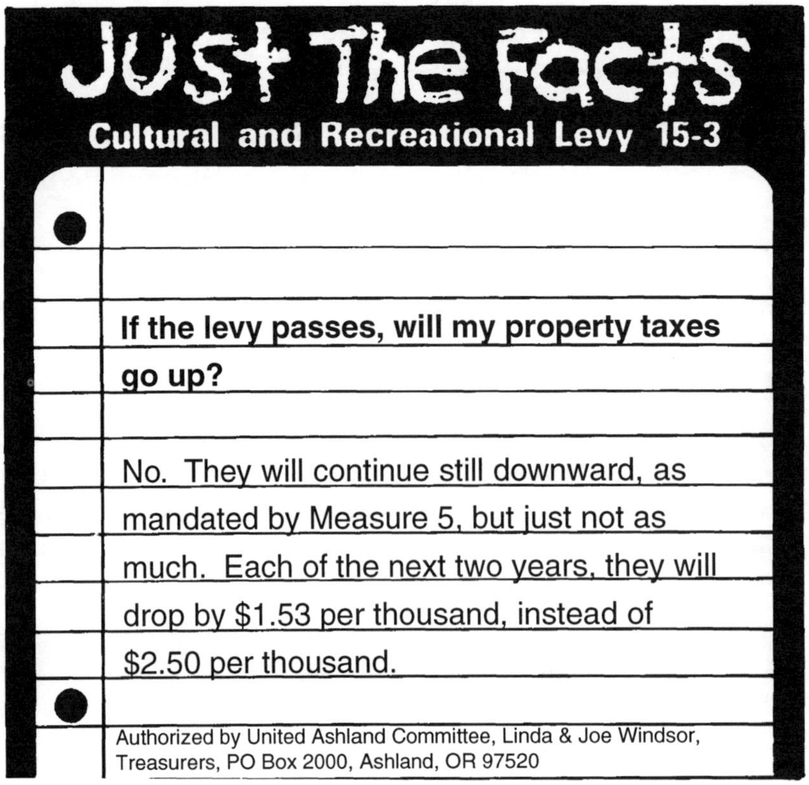

Just The Facts
Cultural and Recreational Levy 15-3

If the levy passes, will my property taxes go up?

No. They will continue still downward, as mandated by Measure 5, but just not as much. Each of the next two years, they will drop by $1.53 per thousand, instead of $2.50 per thousand.

Authorized by United Ashland Committee, Linda & Joe Windsor, Treasurers, PO Box 2000, Ashland, OR 97520

Fig. 10.1 Example of Information Ad

Timing Your Ads

Once your candidate or measure appears in a campaign ad in the paper or on TV or radio, the ads must continue to appear. It will hurt your campaign more than you realize to run some early ads, then take a break before running more ads. Your first ads will make the biggest impression. Choose them carefully. If you start and then stop, it gives the appearance that the campaign is faltering or without funds—that is, support. No one wants to back a losing team.

Once you start a media campaign, work it like the fireworks on the Fourth of July. Start with a little at first, then add more and more, climaxing with the finale just before the election. Your money determines when you can *start* advertising, not when you will end. You always end a day out from the election.

If you are working on a winning campaign, fund raising for ads will get easy. Go to your local paper and talk to the person who sells display ads. Don't forget to ask whether there is a special rate for political ads.

Because most campaigns run their media with greater frequency as they get closer to the election, media buys become scarce. In TV, as with radio, there are just so many seconds in the hour. Unlike a newspaper that can add more pages, TV and radio have limited amounts of time to sell. Depending on the popularity of the show, the time when you might consider a buy is even more restricted. If you do not secure your media buys early, two weeks out, there won't be any left to buy.

That does not mean you have to deliver finished products the day you buy ad time. All of that production can happen later. It does mean that in August/September you are going to buy 30 seconds on the evening news for November 1st and write a check. This is where early endorsements and early money pay off.

Advertising Formats

All political campaigns have a tendency to look messy. There is literature dropped at the voters' doors, lawn signs all over town, and political ads in the paper. If you can organize your efforts and give a sense of continuity and neatness to your particular campaign, by all means do it. If you have a campaign slogan, put it in all your ads, on your lawn signs, and in the brochures. You should have an easily identifiable logo and put it on everything. I use my lawn sign as my logo and I have a miniature made up for canvassers' buttons and as the trademark on my all media ads.

If I am running ads for a candidate, I like the newspaper ads to look a bit like a newspaper story. I will place the candidate's picture as a fairly prominent part of the ad, under which will be the logo. I place a headline of my choosing and then have the copy run alongside the picture. Candidate ads should be no more than three paragraphs, on one subject. Below the copy will be the campaign slogan.

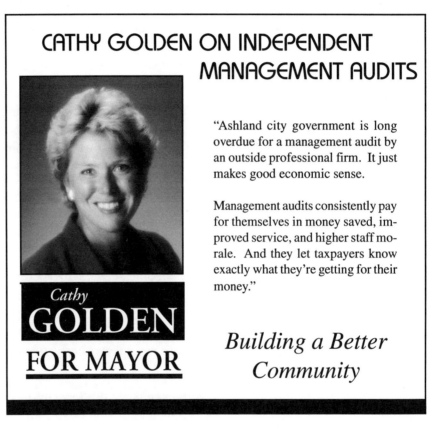

Fig. 10.2 Example of Candidate Ad made to look like a newspaper article

I might have five or six ads of this nature that I rotate in and out with different pictures and text. Generally, I like to run small ads such as a two-by-four, which is two columns wide by four inches. Not only are small ads cheaper, they tend to be placed on top of other ads, directly under newspaper copy. If you have lots of money, you can make the ad any size you want. If properly placed, on the back page for example, large ads can be very effective.

Another effective newspaper ad is an individual testimonial. One campaign I worked on used the same format as outlined previously but took quotations from prominent citizens about the candidate to use as the text. Don't make the mistake of using a picture of the person who is being quoted. It is important to get the candidate's face in front of the public at every opportunity. I have also pulled great lines from various letters-to-the-editor and used them in a large testimonial ad. There might be ten quotations spread out, as well as a picture of the candidate, logo, and slogan. Very effective.

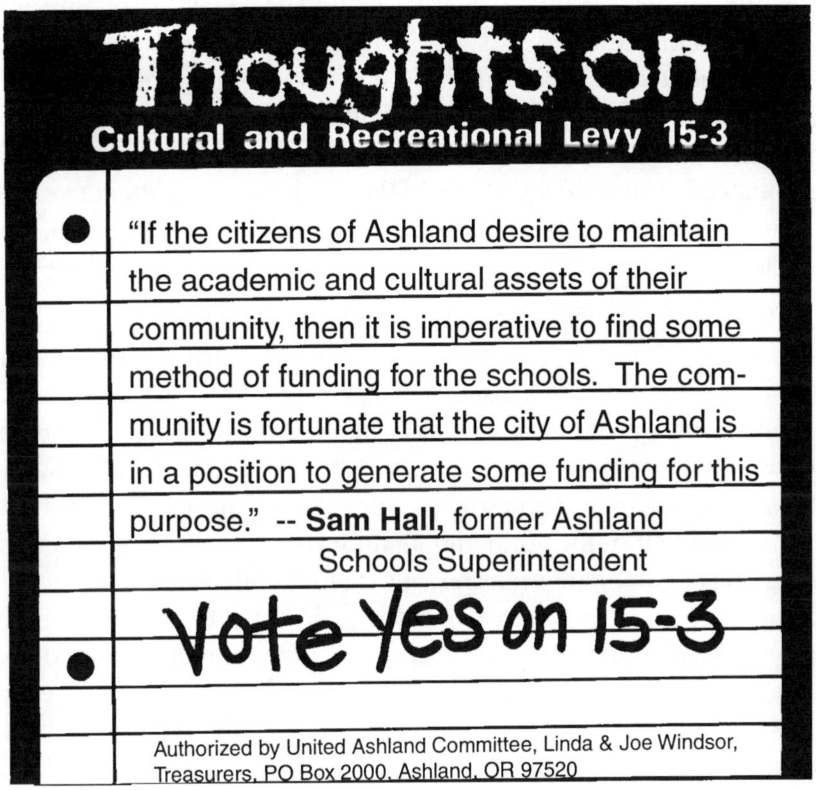

Fig. 10.3 Example of Endorsement Ad

In my first run for mayor, I was characterized as a no-growth candidate. My feeling was that growth itself wasn't the problem, but rather the effect it had on our quality of life. Some would say it is too fine a distinction, but I argued if we did all we could to mitigate the effects of growth, we would probably be OK. One of my small information ads referred to building moratoria as being a result of poor planning for growth. Later, when I was endorsed by the Board of Realtors, I blew up the building moratorium adding a footnote headline saying that the realtors had endorsed me.

By coupling the real estate community's endorsement with my advocacy of good planning, I took the bite out of my opponent's "no-growth" charge and replaced it with a responsible growth idea. If I had not been endorsed by the realtors, I would simply have said, no surprise there.

If you have a ballot or revenue measure being placed before the voters, it is generally best to go for emotion in your ads. You can and should run some information ads, but a better response can often be had with a picture and very little copy. For example, for our "Open Space Plan" we ran ads that juxtaposed pictures of open fields filled with grazing sheep with a more current photo showing the same fields filled with wall-to-wall housing. The caption asked the voter to leave some of the community untouched. Similarly, we ran other ads comparing pictures of the city before and after development. When running a campaign for a school issue (tax base, school board, etc.), we show lots of pictures. Pictures personalize what people are voting on.

I worked on a campaign where we hoped voters would pick up after-school functions to offset a statewide property tax measure that was under-mining school funding. Because of the wording of our City Charter, the city could pick up only programs that would enhance the recreational and cultural aspects of our city and the vicinity. Getting voters to spend additional money for extracurricular activities can be tricky. Many of the activities did not exist when the older half of the voting population were in school. At least 15% of the voters were two generations beyond having children in the schools. We needed to convey the importance of extracurricular activities as a critical part helping our students. To do this we had one ad that juxtaposed two resumes of the same student. One had nothing but an excellent GPA; the other had the GPA plus a list of all her ancillary activities showing involvement and leadership. The caption read: "Which student would you rather hire?" We ran another ad that was identical but said, "Which student is more likely to get into a great college?" Without a lot of print we could get to the heart of the challenges facing our students today if they are to get ahead.

During a campaign to pass a food and beverage tax measure, we were being hit with how it was a tax on the locals one minute and on the tourists the next. The opponents were correct; the tax did reach both locals and tourists. Although the tax was slated to acquire more park land for future generations and fix our ailing sewage treatment plant, we felt these were services that both locals and tourists used. To say this dramatically, we ran an ad with a picture of the city's central plaza on the Fourth of July when more than 30,000 people drop into the city for the day. The caption read: "225,000 visitors each year use our parks, have their bedding laundered, and flush toilets." Through this ad we stayed on our message of parks and waste water treatment plant updates while redirecting the opposition's energy back on them. This tax measure passed. Twice. Emotional ads can be very effective.

"The charm of politics is that dull as it may be in action, it is endlessly fascinating as a rehash."
Eugene McCarthy

Fig. 10.4 Example of Emotional Ad

150,000 VISITORS TO ASHLAND A YEAR:

Photo by Christopher Briscoe

- **FLUSH TOILETS**

- **TAKE SHOWERS**

- **HAVE THEIR SHEETS AND TOWELS LAUNDERED**

This creates considerable sewage flow.

Visitors should share in the sewage solution.

The revenues from Measure 15-1 will come from a good blend of locals AND visitors.

Paid for and authorized by the Good For Ashland! Committee, Hal Cloer, Treasurer, PO Box 0, Ashland, OR.

IT'S GOOD FOR ASHLAND! VOTE YES ON 15-1

Fig. 10.5 Example of Emotional Ad

Endorsements and Endorsement Ads

Endorsements from support groups, editorial boards, and business and community leaders can mean both money and votes for your effort. As you get endorsements, incorporate them into your brochure, newspaper ads, direct mail, TV, and radio. Craft them into press releases and send them to the local papers and newsrooms.

In the media, endorsement ads are examples of the best kind of testimonial ads, and they can take many forms. You can list the hundreds of people who support you, hopefully showing a broad cross section of your community. You can also pull quotations and names from letters-to-the-editor, as indicated earlier, or have a page of logos from businesses that endorse you under a caption.

Campaigns routinely postpone putting together an endorsement ad with hundreds of names until the last minute. Regardless of whether you intend to run one, you should prepare from the beginning as though you will. You can save hours of last-minute phoning if, right from the start, you ask everyone you talk to whether you can use their names in a newspaper endorsement ad. This will not only make producing an endorsement ad much easier, but it tells you whether the person you are contacting is in fact a supporter and how public the person wants to go with his or her support. Some believe that endorsement ads are ineffective. But when you "hear" that your opponent is doing one, suddenly everything gets dropped while your volunteers start calling lists of people who might sign on for a counter ad. This gives your volunteers the impression that the campaign is very disorganized. It also takes time away from canvassing, phone banking, fund raising, and maintaining lawn signs at the end of the campaign when volunteers are stretched to the limit. The last hours of a campaign are precious, so don't needlessly burden yourself with these ads. Take care of it as you go.

In one campaign on which I worked, the candidate said that he didn't want to do an endorsement ad. Accordingly, we never collected names for such an ad. Then at the end of the campaign, his opponent came out with one of the best endorsement ads I have ever seen. The ad had a few great pictures of the opponent doing something wonderful—you know, with babies and dogs, a few very tasteful lines about America that even had me with a lump in my throat—and then one full page of names. A full newspaper page of names. Even if we had started calling then and there and did nothing else until the election, we couldn't have made the 500 calls that it would have required to run a similar ad. The ad went unanswered.

When doing an endorsement ad, keep a separate list of names in a computer or create a field for the endorsement ad sort. This is a time when access to a computer really helps. Being able to sort the endorsement list alphabetically helps you find duplicate names. However, when it comes time to run the endorsement ad—and hopefully you will have hundreds of names— do not put the names in alphabetical order. Random listing of names gets people to read through more of them looking for friends and family, and random order allows you to put your big names in prominent locations, especially at the tops of columns. If you know you are going to do an endorsement ad and you are not using a computer, periodically give the typesetter a list of the names. In the final days of a campaign, when it is likely everyone is going to your typesetter asking for things to be done yesterday, showing up with 450 names on every scrap of paper imaginable makes for the most interesting conversations. Avoid this by planning ahead.

In one campaign, we ran the endorsement ad on shocking yellow paper as a door hanger. At the top front was the candidate logo with a "Join us in voting for [message]." It was followed by hundreds of names. We did an early Saturday canvass, hanging them on all doors in the city.

Letters-to-the-Editor and Free Media

If you don't have the funds for a sustained paid advertising campaign, start by encouraging letters-to-the-editor. This will carry the campaign until the paid advertising can begin. Depending on your area, using the letters-to-the-editor section of the local paper can be a very effective media tool. Such letters show that a voter cares enough about a candidate or ballot measure to take the time to write a letter, get it in an envelope, put a stamp on it, and get it to a paper. Letters-to-the-editor can be the most effective endorsement ads going.

If you are going to use letters-to-the-editor in your campaign effec-tively, you should have someone overseeing that activity. The person in charge needs to call people who have promised to write letters and make sure they get them in.

The coordinator should also be prepared to write several different sample letters to give people guidance and help move them along.

It is important to get letters in early. Early letters get read. Later in the campaign season, readers become numb and rarely read the last-minute opinions of their neighbors. Keep the letters short. A good rule is, one to two paragraphs, one subject. People do not read long letters in the paper. What

"The press always has the last word."

Tom Olbrich

you really want are a lot of short letters that will get you more boldfaced titles that people will notice at a glance. Also short letters are often printed more quickly, and because short letters are great space fillers, they are sometimes printed after the paper has said, "No more letters."

Vote for Daniels

Elle Daniels would be an excellent school board member. Elle has devoted her life to education as a volunteer in the classroom.

We need people in decision making positions who know first-hand what is going on with our children. Elle Daniels has my vote.

C. Golden,
Ashland, OR

Fig. 10.6 Example of Letter-to-the-Editor

Be sure to have your supporters send copies of letters to all of the local papers. You never know who reads what.

Many papers will not print letters received a certain number of days prior to the election. Get this information. Almost everyone likes to procrastinate, and you and your coordinator need to make sure the deadline is met. If you're depending on letters for media advertising, being too late could be fatal to your cause. Keep in mind that, because many papers must first verify authenticity of mailed letters by phone prior to printing, hand carrying the letter means that it gets printed sooner. Also, letters that are typed get printed faster.

Other Free Media Coverage

Most newspapers have a public interest section that lists who is speaking when and where. Look for this section. You will need to find out how often it runs and when the deadlines are. If your candidate is talking or one of your committee members is giving a presentation on your ballot measure, be sure it gets in the community activity section of the paper.

I once saw a notice in a community activity section that a particular candidate would be canvassing that week in a neighboring town. It really got my attention. At first I thought how odd, surely no one cares when or where this person will be canvassing. But to the average person, it appears that the candidate is stomping the beat, making herself available to the regular folks, even if that candidate never makes it to the reader's front door.

Getting on the Front Page and Creating Media Events

When you announce that you will be seeking office, it is important to call all of the press. To get the print, radio, and television media there, you will have to schedule the announcement for the convenience of the media, not for your or your supporters' convenience. Call the local papers to find out their deadlines. Ask what would be the most convenient time for a reporter and photographer to attend your announcement. If you know some of the media cannot attend, have printed news releases delivered to those who will miss the announcement.

As a general rule, I would rather have the print media miss an announcement. Keep in mind that television news crews like to attend these things no earlier than late morning. They all work at night. Getting your face in front of the camera is important. If you can do that, you can cover the print media with a prepared speech and a studio photo. If your announcement is too late for the newspapers to be there, be sure to get them the information they need before they hit deadline. You want your announcement covered everywhere on the same day.

To find a good date and time to announce a candidacy or to kick off a ballot measure campaign, you have to know what else is going on when you plan to announce. You don't want to announce on major holidays because people don't watch the news or read the papers as much on those days. For the same reason, you don't want to announce on a three-day weekend. If it is a nonpartisan race with only a general election, I like to announce in June so that I can participate in the Fourth of July parades. The general rule is to do whatever you can to get your name out in an inexpensive and effective way.

Recently a candidate announced his intention to seek a state legislative office. He said that if people wanted him to, he would run, but that he needed a ground swell to appear. So this guy wants us to beg him to run and support his campaign. People work for a candidate exactly as hard as a candidate works for himself or herself. No one is going to beg. The media barely covered his announcement, figuring he really wasn't serious yet. Bad start.

Press Conference

If there is an opportunity to call a press conference, do it. When I was working on our food and beverage tax campaign, the opposition called a press conference to announce a funding scheme for open space that would make our tax unnecessary. They gathered together a broad range of local interests to support their scheme. To counter, we called a press conference as well.

We also had a broad range of local interests represented at our press conference. We took advantage of the occasion to point out why the funding proposed by the opposition would fall short of the community's needs. We also went one step further and used the press conference as an opportunity to promote our campaign. We were, therefore, not only able to undo any damage the opposition's proposal might have caused, but we used the opportunity to advance our own campaign goals. We kept our campaign message out front. Politics is motion: take energy that is coming at you and redirect it at your opposition.

In general, I do not invite the media to coffees, fund-raisers, or other special events. Not only am I worried that the event may be poorly attended and the coverage will work against us, but I have also noticed that people want this time with the candidate. If the media is there, it gives a sense that everything is staged and those in attendance are merely props. Do not, however, hesitate to include the media if a big name politician is willing to endorse you or your measure. I once worked for a candidate who chose to turn down the Governor's endorsement and visit because he felt that the Governor was not all that popular, especially in our district. That was a mistake. A big political figure can get you the only page of the paper that is not for sale—the front page—not to mention all of the leads of the evening news.

There are a number of other tricks you can use to get on the front page of the papers. Challenging your opponent to a series of debates is a time-honored way to get local front-page coverage. Another way to capture media interest is to announce that you are challenging your opponent to campaign on a limited budget. If you issue the challenge, you get to come up with the amount; so set it where you can live with it, but doubt your opponent can.

If you're an incumbent, this can really work to your advantage. In small city elections, incumbents are better known and don't need to spend as much as outsiders to get their names out. Because the public thinks incumbents are compromised, this has the appearance making them look more pure.

Press Events

Whenever possible create press events. This is where your research can really pay off. Use what the opposition is claiming and then look for inconsistencies in past actions, voting records, and money trails. Dribble this information to the press so that it comes out in increments. Look for where your opposition is getting money and support, and if this is inconsistent with their message, get this information to the press. Look for the opposition to hook and then hammer them. For example, you are running against an incumbent who claims to be a clean air advocate. You point out how his voting record is inconsistent with that claim, knowing full well that there were other favorable clean air votes that he will pull out to make you look silly. That is OK; the hook has been taken. If he doesn't respond, your accusation stands, but if he does, you have a hammer. In this case you hook him with the clean air vote and then hammer him with a history of contributions from polluting companies and other non-air quality votes of his that would indicate he is bought and sold by these companies. This is where your homework pays off. Make sure the opposing campaign is true and honest to the voting record and message.

If you find ten inconsistencies with the opposing campaign, use them for ten press releases or press conferences, not one press conference with a list of ten. Use supporters to point out your strengths as well as the problems with the opposing candidate or measure. For example, the Board of Realtors endorses you, an anti-growth candidate. Call a press conference for this announcement and help the realtors with a reason. In their endorsement they should include not only why they endorse you but also why they are *not* endorsing your opposition. Negative campaigning from a third party is best because it doesn't come from your campaign.

Take advantage of events that are already happening, like the 4th of July Parade. Show up for events that are likely to get media coverage, and let the press know that you will be there, for example, if a special speaker is scheduled to talk at a regular meeting of the AARP.

In Summary

1. Create news through research, package it in finite pieces, and get it to the press.

2. Appear at events.

3. Challenge your opponent to debates or to keep within campaign spending limits.

4. Use ammunition coming at you and redirect it at the opposition in press releases and press conferences.

5. If you are an incumbent, create events by attending others' events.

6. Create a media event when you announce your candidacy or campaign kickoff.

7. Create media events with your campaign activities. For example, let the press know that 100 people covered your city in two hours on Saturday.

8. Use endorsements as media events.

Fielding Questions from the Press

If you are calling press conferences or thinking up ways to get on the front page of the papers, you need to consider that the press will ask questions that you may not feel ready to answer. The best advice I can give is that, if you're not ready to answer, don't.

Whenever the press calls me on the phone with a question I have not considered or feel unprepared to answer, I tell them that I am in the middle of something and ask if I can call back. I ask them the latest time I can call them so they don't miss deadline. If it is a complicated issue, and they give me a couple of days, I take the time so I can do some research before I call them back. If they say they are on deadline and need it right now, I say I'll call back in five minutes. Even a short amount of time can be enough to get your bearings straight. Call your media advisor, campaign manager, partner, or supporter with specific expertise, and come up with an answer. It is a good idea to write down specific points you want to touch on before you call the reporter back. Make these short and quotable and deliver them with spontaneity.

One important note: if you ask a reporter to "go off the record," the reporter must agree or else you are not officially off the record. For example, if I am about to share something with a newspaper reporter as a way of giving background, and I do not want my name to appear with the information, I will say, "May we go off the record?" I then wait for the reporter to say "yes" or "no." It does not work to say something and then tell the reporter, "and by the way, that was off the record," or "please do not print that."

I cannot stress how important this issue is. Because tempers flair when you are in the midst of a political campaign, think how what you say or do will read the next day in the paper and choose your words carefully. I hear people say that the papers took their comments out of context or distorted what they said. I have rarely found that to be the case. More often, I have wished I had been misquoted.

Radio and Television

While I would not begin to try to lay out a television or radio campaign for you here, I will summarize some important points to keep in mind if you are going to design a television or radio campaign.

1.   This kind of advertising requires a great deal of money, more than you can imagine if you are to do it effectively. Be prepared. Do not start until you have enough money to see your ads through to election day.

2.   As I said before, *buy early*. There is just so much air time for sale, and other campaigns will compete with you for that time. If you wait to get your air time until just before the election, there will be none to buy.

3.   Treat TV and radio like canvassing. Do not put ads on programs watched by people who will be voting for you anyway. Similarly, do not advertise on programs where you will activate "no" votes for your cause. Ask to see some of the demographics on those who watch particular programs. Radio and TV stations know exactly who listens and watches what and when. Don't spend money preaching to the choir. Concentrate your efforts on the souls that can be saved, not on the saints and certainly not on the sinners.

4.   Use radio. Radio is inexpensive to produce and a great buy. It is perhaps the biggest bang for the buck.

5.   Radio and TV are very different art forms. Do not have the same people who do your TV, do your radio.

6.   Ask for media preferred rates.

Consider doing ten-second TV spots. These are relatively inexpensive to produce and air. Also, because of their length, they get better placement when air time is at a premium.

Bumper Stickers and Buttons

Bumper stickers are an inexpensive way to familiarize your name or ballot measure with the community. Whereas bumper stickers are predominantly used in large city, county, state, or federal races, they can also be quite effective in the small election simply because they continue to be a novelty there.

This is one time I would move from my strong recommendation of placing your campaign logo on all your materials. Ideally you want your candidate or measure before the voters, nothing more. Bumper stickers are small and hard to read, so clarity is what is important. In one campaign we placed the logo along with the name. Even though the logo was written in a modified fashion, it was still difficult to read.

An added bonus is that bumper stickers are occasionally left on cars if a candidate wins, giving the community the impression that the individual is well liked in office. People who like to display bumper stickers are often willing to kick in a dollar or two to buy them.

Two words of caution. First, should you decide to print bumper stickers, be sure to print them on removable stock. If people know they will easily come off after the election, they are more inclined to place one. Second, urge people to drive courteously while displaying your name on their cars. If they are rude on the road, the only thing the other driver will remember is your name.

Buttons are walking testimonials or endorsements. If supporters actually wear them, it further serves the goal of getting your name in front of the voting public. My experience is that very few people put them on each day, and they tend to be added clutter and expense. However, since all canvassers should have some sort of official identification with the campaign, this is what I recommend:

At a stationery store, purchase a box of the type of plastic name holders used at conventions or meetings. Ask the graphic design artist who put together the lawn-sign logo to make a miniature version of the logo for the plastic badges. Also ask the designer to lay out enough of these to fill a sheet of paper. Reproduce on card stock as many as you think you will need. Keep the original to make more throughout the campaign. Cut out your miniature lawn-sign logos and slide them into the plastic holders. After the campaign you can reuse the plastic name badges.

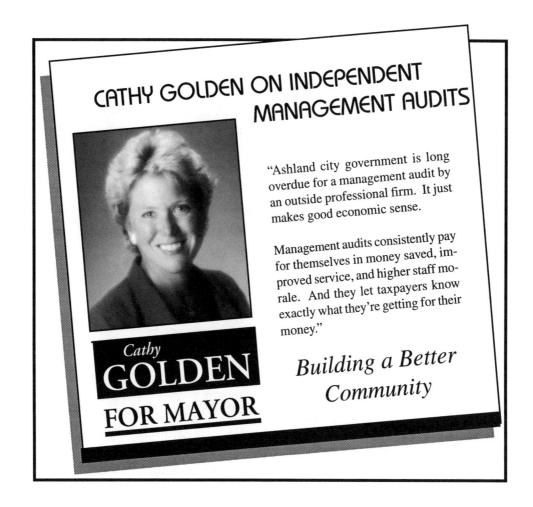

Fig. 10.7 Example of Ad made more striking by adding shading and placing at angle in a box

Chapter 11

The Candidate

In this chapter

Packaging the Candidate

Stay on Your Message

Outsider's Campaign vs. Incumbent's Campaign

Debates

Fielding Negative Questions

Developing Your Public Speaking Skills

Speaking Engagements

Thank-you Notes

Once you declare your intentions to run for office, you become part of the public domain. You are fair game for just about any criticism people might feel inclined to level at you. Should someone write a letter with an outright lie in it, you essentially have little recourse. You can defend, but you cannot sue. Some political analysts think candidates should ignore attacks and lies. However, far more think that unanswered allegations imply truth. Either way it is a problem. You can defend yourself, but when you decide to run, you give up your right to whine. It is great preparation for office.

This chapter is about projecting a positive image before the voters and thereby minimizing the potential nit-picking that the public might do. You will also find suggestions on how to redirect negative questions at your opponent, turning the ammunition back on him or her. As a candidate, this is not a time to be defensive. Take criticism as a gift and an opportunity.

Prior to declaring my intentions to run for mayor, I was at a picnic with my family in a nearby city. The Historic Society was sponsoring the event on a glorious summer evening on the lawn in front of a museum. The speaker was

"Common sense is genius dressed in its working clothes."
Ralph Waldo Emerson

the Secretary of State, and within a few years would be our first woman governor. I remember being wowed by her speech and filled with pride at the prospect of joining ranks in the elected arena with women of her capability.

As I was eating, a friend shared a comment she had just heard about me. A woman had said, "How can she ever hope to run a city if she can't leave her children at home?" I was stunned, enraged, offended, and more. But once I calmed down, I thought about her criticism. If she felt this way at an *outdoor picnic,* imagine the criticism at a more formal event. Rather than react in a defensive way, I realized that my actions were more potent than my words. If I were elected, I could lead by example and thereby serve as a role model for young women in the community. However, if I moved off my campaign message to beat up potential voters on the double standards that exist in society, I might never hold a position of leadership, serve as a role model, and accomplish the programs that prompted me to run in the first place. I did not let the criticism distract me. I also choose to not drag my children through the political process with me. I would add that children need a life of their own and are better off not serving as political props.

Packaging the Candidate

A political candidate is selling a lot more than political views. People are looking for an individual who will represent their community, city, school, or county in a professional way. Elected officials fulfill the role of continually answering with the public trust. If the community believes in the candidate, then they'll believe that their money is in good hands. To meet voter expectations, the candidate must always look the part.

If the candidate's clothes have a spot, no matter how small, change clothes. A candidate should not have any holes in his or her clothes; shoes should be polished; clothes buttoned; and the buttons not pulling or strained from a poor fit.

Because people associate weight loss with happiness and success, an overweight candidate may choose to diet and lose weight. Canvassing can really help in this area. Whatever improvements can be made in a candidate's appearance and dress, make them. Attention to appearance will project a positive image, and the candidate will look and feel the part. The candidate and the campaign cannot afford to cut corners on personal appearance and dress. A crumpled look may be endearing at home but not on someone running for public office. Inattention to personal appearance translates into inattention to detail and incompetence.

Dress in a consistent style. This gives the community the impression that you are stable and know who you are. Do not do things out of character.

"No man, for any considerable period, can wear one face to himself, and another to the multitude, without finally getting bewildered as to which may be the truth."
Nathaniel Hawthorne

We all remember the picture of Michael Dukakis in the military tank. Cowboy hat and boots worked for Ronald Reagan but not for Bill Clinton. Behave and dress in a way that is consistent with who you are.

Recently a candidate for a mayor's race in a large metropolitan city countered accusations that he was "uptight" by jumping into the shower with a couple of radio disc jockeys. Voters want stability in office and run from those who act out of character or in an unpredictable manner. If someone accuses you of being uptight, say that's right, that's the kind of person who can do what this city needs. Then move back to your message with specific examples of what the city needs and how you will meet the challenge.

Manners Matter

As important as they are, there is more to looking the part of a serious public servant than dress and appearance. The candidate must adopt the kind of manners a mother would be proud of. Political candidates do not chew with their mouths open or chew gum. Cover your mouth when you yawn. Recently, a U.S. Representative, running for the U.S. Senate, called and asked to meet with me to "touch base." During our 45-minute meeting he must have yawned five times, and not once did he cover his mouth. I cannot remember what we talked about, but I remember his uvula.

If appearing as a dinner speaker, the candidate should eat at home prior to the event or eat only moderately at the event. The candidate cannot afford to have a stomach upset from nervous energy and certainly can't afford to burp through the speech. In general, eating and meeting voters don't mix well.

Bring along a sweater or light jacket to cover up nervous perspiration if need be. Wear deodorant and clean shirts. Previously worn clothes can carry body odor that might be activated with nervous perspiration. Bring breath mints, but don't be a candidate that pulls out the little bottle of breath freshener and squirts it mid-sentence. In fact, avoid all public grooming: hair combing, lipstick, and the like. Avoid problems by thinking ahead. For instance, when I get nervous, my mouth gets dry, so I always go to the podium with a glass of water.

As I said before, a woman candidate should leave her children at home. Besides being more focused, voters need to see her in a professional role. It is difficult for many people to accept a woman as a leader if their only image is one of children clinging to her. This is absolutely *not* true for men. In fact, men are given bonus points for being seen with their children. Society assumes men are professional, and seeing a man with his children gives the voters the idea that they are getting a glimpse into his private life. He seems warmer.

Groomers

Given the importance of image, it may be a good idea to get a "groomer" for the campaign. I generally have a friend whose only campaign job is to let me know how I look and to make suggestions on what I should wear and how to better project my image. In both of my campaigns for mayor, I had a groomer who proved to be invaluable. When I was to be on Public Access Television in a debate with my two male opponents, my groomer advised me to dress conservatively. One opponent showed up dressed very casually and looked less than professional to the television audience.

The next debate of the campaign was covered by the media, but not broadcast live. My groomer predicted that my principal opponent, having looked casual for the Public Access Television debate, would dress conservatively for this one. He advised me to wear my hair differently and dress in a brightly colored dress I had rarely been seen in. The idea was that I should stand out to the live audience.

I selected a colored dress from the depths of my closet. My opponent, as predicted, wore a three-piece black suit and appeared quite intense, severe, even funereal. Because the debate was before a live audience, I had time prior to the debate to say hello, chat with members of the crowd, and enjoy myself. My appearance was friendly, and I was clearly having a good time. My opponent did not smile and seemed out of place, strapped in his television armor. The difference between us was dramatic, and the debate proved to be a turning point in the campaign.

Pick and choose your events carefully. Do not say yes to every coffee or speaking engagement offer that may come your way. Think ahead where you intend to spend time and energy and go where the votes are. Take into consideration the personality of your candidate. For example, minimize the amount of time in public for the candidate who is awkward in the crowd.

Stay on Your Message

Don't let your opponent pull you off message. Ever.

The look of the candidate is important as voters need to be able to identify with him or her. However, the candidate and team must know who will support the candidate and why. The reason that people vote a specific way will become the basis for your campaign message. Develop that message to build relationships between you and the voters. A poll can really help here.

"Too bad that all the people who know how to run the country are busy driving taxicabs and cutting hair."
George Burns

List all the positives of your candidate and why the team feels voters will support this individual. That list might include programs the candidate has been involved in, stands on controversial issues, prior votes (if a previous office holder), vision, character, and experience. It might be nothing more than a clear list of issues and beliefs that the candidate embraces.

You must also develop a list of issues and concerns that might hurt the candidate's support. (There should be a fair amount of overlap from the positives list to the negatives list.) It is this list that you will use to prepare the candidate for negative questions and formulate strategies to defuse negative perceptions. For example, if the candidate has an image of being slick, the team sends him to neighborhood meetings where he can shine as one of the crowd. This requires a candidate open to observation and criticism, a close campaign team to develop the campaign message, and people willing to do research on your opponent.

Once you have developed your campaign message and strategy, stick to it. When hit by your opponent, respond and move the discussion right back to your message. When appropriate, go after your opponent's campaign inconsistencies and weaknesses.

As I have said before, the campaign team will work only as hard as a candidate or campaign leader. So work hard. Also the public, besides looking for a community representative and leader, is observing everything during the campaign: your stand on issues, your presence and composure, your appearance, your ability to answer their questions. In particular the public is looking for how well you react under pressure and how hard you work to get into office. That will tell them something about whether they can expect you to keep your head and work hard once you are in office.

While looking professional, minding your manners, working hard, and being on message, you must find some way to minimize stress. One way is to listen to your campaign team. Another is to do nothing which, after being done, leads you to tell a lie. Finally, always look like you are having a good time. For additional information on reducing stress, see the "Debates" section later in this chapter.

Outsider's Campaign vs. Incumbent's Campaign

Outsiders

If you are in government already, you are an insider; if not, you're an outsider. Insiders and outsiders typically run very different campaigns because the voters expect the insider to defend what government is doing and the outsider to challenge it with a fresh outlook. In reality, however, skillful

"Know who you are before others find out."
My Mom

politicians who have been in office for years have, when the need arises, waged outsider campaigns against first-time candidates. Insider/outsider is as much a state of mind as a fact. Whatever the actual status of the candidate, insider and outsider campaigns require distinctly different campaign strategies.

To run an outsider's campaign, you must first legitimize yourself through establishment endorsement (no matter how tangential the endorsement might be) and you must go after the system. But be careful, as Jimmy Carter learned, never to attack the system in such a way that it will be difficult to work with people afterwards.

Attacks on the system are effective if they plant seeds of doubt about how things are being done or where attention and public money are being focused. You cannot just throw complaints against a wall to see what sticks. Instead, know what you're talking about. Find out how things have worked or not worked and explain them to the voters. Remember, you must sound like a potential office holder rather than a malcontent. That requires solutions, not just complaints. This is where the homework really pays off.

Prior to my first run for mayor I went to the local college and checked out ten years of city council minutes and read them all. I also checked out every current report on every system where the city had a consultant study. I read the city's comprehensive plan and the downtown plan. It put me at a decided advantage. Simply because it was all so fresh in my mind, I could recall the information more quickly. Incumbents who live through the reports while in office will find it difficult to recall the details. I know that I would have trouble remembering specifics of reports that have come out since I took office.

Incumbents

If you are an incumbent, you must show that the average citizen still supports you and how, working cooperatively with other elected officials, you have made the system better. That does not mean that you need to defend every stupid government program that went wrong during your tenure in office. It does mean, however, that you point out major battles that were fought and won and why the area you represent is a better place because of your efforts. I might add that it is a good idea not to take all the credit here and, instead, list accomplishments in office as a result of you and your fellow elected officials working together. Remember, after the election you will hopefully be working with them once more.

The best strategy for an incumbent is to make clear what you did and why. Although you not actually use the word, stick close to a theme of leadership. Make your record the focal point of the campaign.

"Enlightenment will be extinguished . . . unless applied . . . to the machinery of political and legislative action."
Margaret Sanger

Your Opponent

You may breathe a sigh of relief when you discover that you are unopposed in your election or groan when you find that at the last minute someone has filed to run against you. However, an opponent in any campaign is a blessing. Without an opponent, your race will be ignored by the press, and the programs and issues you want to get before the voters will be that much more difficult and expensive to get there. If you are involved in a hotly contested race, the press will more likely provide front-page coverage, which greatly reduces the amount of advertising you will have to buy.

If you have a primary race in which you are unopposed, you may never build the momentum and party support that are necessary to win the general. Do not lament if someone declares against you. Thank your lucky stars and organize a great campaign. Bring forward programs you want to begin or maintain, and use the election as a mandate to muscle these into place. Use the election as a reminder of who you are, what you stand for, and as a rallying point to get people behind your efforts.

While working on ballot measures, I discovered that some voters need something to vote *for* while others need something to vote *against*. Average voters watch the debate unfold in the paper and on the news. They listen to see who makes sense and who doesn't. Some get outraged by inane arguments from the opposition and decide to vote for your cause although they normally would not, given their voting proclivities. Without the mis-steps and mis-statements of your opposition, you might never get the necessary votes to push your campaign over the top. However, the drawback of an opponent is that negative campaigning might follow. The discussion in the next section will advise on how to best head this off and deal with it firmly.

Debates

Don't use debates to attack your opponent; rather tell what you know and would do once elected.

If you are well prepared, political debates are surprisingly easy and great fun. As a political candidate, you should welcome the showiness of debates, the pressure, and the opportunity to get your opinions in front of voters. When you have successfully positioned yourself as a candidate, people recognize who you are and what you do. It makes sense to them.

The central rule of debating is that you want the voters to know more following the debate than they did before, so come armed with lots of information. To get ready for a political debate, choose about eight to ten subjects that are of interest to you and/or the community. You should include issues that are part of your campaign platform. For each of the subjects you

"If you run from a ghost, it will chase you forever."
Irish Proverb

have chosen, list the information and points that you feel are relevant on one side of a 5x8 index card. Use only one card per subject and only one side of the card.

For example, development in the forest interface is of great concern in my community. As an incumbent I would list on one card all that government (with my help) has done to limit development. I would also list concerns of fire danger, and what government, again with my help, is doing to make the forest safer. If I were running an outsider's campaign, for the same subject I would list all that is being done, how that is not enough, what has gone wrong (being specific), and exactly what I would do. The information is just listed, not written out. The idea is to be very familiar with the information before the debate and to use the cards to focus what you want to talk about.

Once you have the subject cards filled out, choose a separate color for each card and color a single stripe along the top of each card in a particular color. For example, your card for budget issues might be red; for forest interface, brown; for park issues, green; for recycling, yellow; for air quality, blue; for transportation, black; and so on. Once color coded, the appropriate card can be skimmed at a glance and be discretely in front of you without your letting people know that not all your information came right off the top of your head. By color coding in advance, you can avoid disorienting yourself looking through all the cards to find the one you want. Once you have the information card you need for a particular subject on top of the stack, you can glance at it while looking around the audience. You should appear to be collecting your thoughts rather than reading the cards.

Do not kid yourself that you can guess all the subjects or questions that will be asked in a debate. You will undoubtedly prepare for areas that never get a question. Even so, with the preparation done ahead of time, you will be much more relaxed and "on" during the debate. Be sure to bring extra blank cards to jot down thoughts during the debate. This will help you remember on rebuttal what you want to say.

Familiarize yourself with any ballot measures coming before the voters or any initiative petitions being circulated. Either the press or your opponent may ask your position, so have a clear idea of where you stand and why.

Fielding Negative Questions

Think of everything as a gift or opportunity.

You will very likely get nasty questions and innuendoes during a debate. Look at such questions as your opportunity to show how well you respond under fire. People know that being subjected to negativity is part of

"The way I see it, if you want the rainbow, you gotta put up with the rain."
     Dolly Parton

serving in public office, and they will want to see how you handle it. Never be defensive. If possible, be humble and a little self-effacing. If you can come up with a little joke that turns the attack to your advantage, so much the better. Find anything that uses the ammunition of the opposition and redirects it at them. If you redirect attacks, it is important to do so with class, without sounding defensive, and with poise. This is your opportunity to sound smart. Being quick on your feet is not a function of IQ but of preparedness.

Your campaign committee should help you list everything that is a weakness: every vote, every mis-statement, every missed meeting, all of it. They should also list everything on which your candidate may appear vulnerable: past voting records, who is paying for the campaign, special interest support, inconsistencies in what he/she says and does. Once this level of homework is done, you will be much more comfortable.

Fatal Flaws

One way to prepare yourself for attacks is to sit with your campaign team and brainstorm on every possible negative question that might come your way. Practice responding to questions concerning your weaknesses. This is especially important if you are working on a ballot measure. Listing the "fatal flaws" of your candidate or measure allows discussion within your support group where the team can deliberate the best possible responses. According to topic, these responses may be placed on your 5x8 cards for handy reference during the debate. Even if the attack is not *exactly* what your team predicted, this level of preparation lends comfort and organization to the candidate or speaker's bureau. The result will be better responses in high-pressure situations.

Let me give you some examples of how to capitalize on negative questions. The last time I ran for mayor, I met criticism of city budget increases by explaining that I was the only member of the budget committee who voted "no" on the last budget. Later in the campaign, my opponent pointed out (during a debate) that when this same budget came before the city council for final approval, the council vote was split. He went on to point out that I failed to cast the tie-breaking "no" vote and instead voted "yes." Why, he asked, if I was so opposed to the budget, during the budget process, was I unwilling to vote "no" at the council level?

You can imagine my surprise. Until that moment, I had forgotten that, when the budget came before the council, two members were away and two for odd reasons voted "no." That left only two voting "yes." As Mayor, I was to cast the deciding vote. As I went to the podium to respond, I pulled out my color-coded budget card.

"If you don't make waves, you're not paddling."
Ted Nugent

From the card, I was able to outline the exact issues on which I had concern as a budget committee member. After relating those concerns to the audience, I explained that I lost my appeal to the budget committee to delve into the issues further and explained that the budget was ultimately adopted by the committee. Having been outvoted at the committee level, I suggested to the audience that it would not be right to, in effect, veto the budget as the Mayor. Therefore, I voted to put in place the will of the majority of the committee and council, even if I personally disagreed with some provisions of the budget.

My opponent, because I was prepared, gave me what I could not get on my own. He gave me the opportunity to show that I had good reasons to vote against the budget during the budget process and that I was willing to set aside my differences with the budget process after losing the vote. As an incumbent I was able to demonstrate that I was still willing to challenge the process and yet be a team player.

Another illustration: At a debate one opponent brought up a program that I had initiated to clear fuel (dead and dying brush) from the forest interface using volunteers. He cited how the program had been a miserable failure, placing the city at great risk of potential litigation due to possible worker injury. I picked up my forest card and took the microphone. I said that while the outcome of the program had been different from first envisioned, it raised community awareness of mitigating fire danger. Moreover, the voters needed to make a decision for the future. Did they want leadership that never tried anything out of fear of failure or leadership that solved problems creatively at the risk of an occasional partial success.

By using this attack as a gift, I was able to direct attention to the limited success of the program and then shift back to my message, which was strong, creative leadership. Leadership willing to take risks.

Another approach to leading or negative questions is the "Yeah, so?" answer. For example, the opposition might say, "Since you became Mayor, the city has acquired more and more programs that should be run by the private sector." Your "Yeah, so?" response might be, " I'm sorry. How is this a problem? The proof is in the pudding. We are extraordinarily successful at providing a broad range of outstanding programs, while saving the taxpayers money." While you may not use these exact words, this is the tone.

Attacks Can Backfire

I think it is somewhat unpredictable to hit your opponent during a debate. Do it carefully. Here is an example of how it can backfire: I worked for a candidate whose opponent, an incumbent, was receiving lots of PAC

"I don't care if he did it or not, just get him to deny it."
Lyndon Johnson

money. My candidate wanted to hit the incumbent for taking special interest money. Because the campaign team had heard rumors that the incumbent had a story to die for whenever he was hit on PAC money, the campaign team felt an attack was dangerous.

At the next debate, however, our candidate went after the credibility of the incumbent based on the PAC money coming in. Our candidate implied that the incumbent was bought and paid for because so much of his money came from PACs and so little from citizens. True to the rumors, the opponent stood up and said that when he was first elected, a supporter who had given a large contribution to his campaign visited his office at the capital. According to the story, the contributor was looking for a particular vote on a bill and felt that the size of the campaign contribution warranted this vote. Our opponent went on to say that after hearing the demand, he went to the bank and took out a personal loan to pay back the contributor. He concluded by saying that no one owned his vote.

In about thirty seconds our opponent not only killed the whole PAC money attack, but showed that he was poor like everyone else in the room— he had to take out a personal loan to payoff the contributor—and that he had integrity. In hindsight, this attack would have taken on new meaning if our campaign had been able to point out other campaign contributions and votes that appeared to follow that money.

Nevertheless in debates, you never know how your opponent will turn an attack around. So, unless I have concrete information, I try not to attack unless it is impromptu, on rebuttal, and my opponent is leading with his chin.

I'll give an example of an opponent leading with his chin. In one debate an incumbent complained that his hands were tied because the opposite party occupied the state house, senate, and governor's seat. The opposing candidate should have stood up and said, "Well, given that my opponent confesses he can do nothing for us, why don't we bring in someone who can." He could then have listed all the ways he was working for and with state government to get things done for the local voters. If people lead with their chins, you can't let it go.

Developing Your Public Speaking Skills

In my first run for mayor, during my first debate, I was elated, excited about what was ahead of me, charged up, and well armed with information. When it was over, I thought I did a great job, and so when someone from the audience came up to me afterwards and handed me a slip of paper, I was certain it was some sort of commitment to get involved in my campaign. The

"Be optimistic. When going after Moby Dick, bring along tartar sauce."
Life's Little Instruction Book

paper said: "You said 'um' 48 times during your speech and the question and answer period that followed. Why don't you join us at Toastmasters?"

As you progress in a campaign, you will gradually get better at public speaking. I have been Mayor for seven years now, and I still get butterflies before a speech; I don't care how perfunctory it is or how young the audience. After years of making speeches, here are the techniques, as well as the tricks that I have learned that work for me.

1. Arrive a few minutes early to get a feel of the audience and the room.

2. Before you go in, sit in the car to go over your speech or talk. You will neither have the time nor inclination to do it once you are inside.

3. When asked a question, answer it. I have an unfortunate tendency to drift into a stream-of-consciousness thing. One thing reminds me of another and another and another. Avoid that.

4. Have fun. Remember you are on stage. This is your moment. Enjoy it.

5. Lose the "um's" and "you know's." Silence can be a moment to gather power. Never underestimate its force.

6. Have some notes about what you are going to say, even if it is a short speech and one you have given a million times. I remember once I was asked to speak at the outdoor Shakespearean Theater with a standing room capacity of around 1000. I had never spoken to such a large group, under lights, or on a stage like that. I walked out and could not remember one line of my two-minute, memorized speech. Not one. I stood there for what seemed like an hour waiting for it to come to me. Nothing. Finally with no hope of it coming back, I looked down at my notes. The first line triggered the speech and out it came. Even if you think you won't need them, bring along some notes.

7. Make your speech fun for others to hear. Include something in it to make them feel proud or appreciated. Throw in some self-deprecating humor. I once watched a candidate give a speech at a Rotary Club meeting. She got up bemoaning the fact that one more mill had closed. It would have been much more effective had she stood up and said: "In Jackson County, small business is big business." She could have followed that up with examples, most of whom were

"The palest ink is better than the most retentive memory."
Old Chinese Proverb

sitting in the room. She also could have pointed out how the success of communities like ours is dependent upon the volunteerism and commitment of organizations such as the Rotary Club. Again give examples. People hate to hear candidates whine. Avoid it.

One speech I gave as mayor was to the Annual Conference of the Engineers of Oregon. I am the daughter of an engineer, and I'm certain my son has all the makings of one. Back then when I got home from work, late at night, my son, six at the time, would call me to his bed. Silly me, I thought it was for a kiss. Instead he would turn on the light, and out from under his bed came the most bizarre contraptions I had ever seen. He would then say, "If I could just have a little piece of electrical tape. . . ." I told this story to the Engineers of Oregon with the tone of, "You don't know how your mothers suffered." I then pulled out of a bag three or four examples of my son's handiwork. It was great fun.

8. I try to add history to my speeches. Some people know the background of their town, but many don't. Call seniors or local historians for ideas.

9. Focus on friends in the audience. I gave a speech once while I was in the middle of a really horrible campaign for a money measure I was personally putting forward. In the audience was one of the opponents, making faces and otherwise distracting me. It had to be the worst speech of my career. Now I look for friendly faces and focus on them.

10. Use quotations, jokes, and anecdotes. Although there are exceptions, I usually do not tell jokes but rather incorporate jokes as funny stories within a speech. This is where self-deprecating humor works.

For example, at a speech to the Oregon Nurses Association, I followed two women who were not nurses but rather children of nurses. Although I had not thought of this while I wrote my speech, I shared that I too was the daughter of a nurse. An Operating Room nurse. I told them that OR nurses are the only people I know who wash their hands before and after they go to the bathroom. Even my mom laughs at this because it's true. Give people something of yourself.

I collect quotations and incorporate wherever possible. There are many books out now that offer up food for thought in quotations.

Look for them and incorporate them in your speeches. Modify them so they are your own words or fit the moment.

11. Share experiences that happened to you on the campaign trail. "The other day while I was canvassing. . ." can be an effective way to make known that you canvass and care what voters think, plus it provides an opportunity to communicate an important idea that is part of your platform.

12. Save correspondence that is entertaining and incorporate it in your speech. My favorite is a letter from a supporter telling me I need to wear more makeup. I never reveal the author's name in this situation.

13. Target your audience with the campaign message.

14. Give your speech to yourself in the mirror or have a supporter videotape a speech and have the campaign team watch and critique it.

Speaking Engagements

I will state the obvious here. Look for opportunities to speak before groups. You need to get your name and face known to the public if you are a candidate, and you need to get your cause before the public if you are working for a measure. With that said, it is just as important to protect the candidate's time from too many activities with marginal returns. Look for speaking opportunities where the audience should be receptive to your campaign message. Focus on the saveables.

When organizing campaigns for ballot measures, I set up a committee of supporters whose sole job is that of a speakers' bureau. If it is a county-wide proposition or measure, the speakers' bureau might be quite large. In an individual city, this committee may be as small as two. Regardless of the size, their job is to seek opportunities to speak and make sure someone is there from the committee to explain the ballot measure and answer questions in a knowledgeable way.

A speakers' bureau is a terrific way of publicly involving big name people who want to be aligned with a campaign, yet lack the skills to work as a campaign committee member. It is also good for the ballot measure. Whereas an election with a candidate depends on that candidate and his or her stands to build relationships with the voters, ballot measures often encompass only one idea. With a ballot measure, the people who attach their name to it create the relationship. You might have the president of the college, the president of the Rotary Club, the mayor, the leaders of every church, and

"The final days are the longest."
Bill Meulemans

so on. Each of these people brings a following. Their names have grown to represent something in the community, and it is their reputations that draw the vote.

Thank-you Notes

Whereas this chapter has dealt primarily with style and appearance, there is one overlooked area that goes a long way in a campaign—the thank-you note. I cannot stress how important "thank-you" notes are. Send them often and not just for money. I like to have half sheets of a high quality paper printed with a letterhead from my computer, and I use matching envelopes. If you have the money, let a print shop do this for you in a different color ink. Blue is very nice on off-white. Jot off a quick thank-you in your own hand to those who put in a little extra effort, those who gave you the coffee, those who donated items for your special event, those who called to turn people out for an event.

Chapter 12

The Campaign Flow-chart

In this chapter

Building Your Campaign Flow-chart
Example of Campaign Flow-chart

You have now almost completed reading this handbook, and based on your time, resources, and volunteer base, you have decided what campaign activities you are capable of doing. You are now ready to create a campaign flow-chart which actually marks the beginning of your campaign. Start by listing the tasks you need to complete before election. Those might be canvassing, brochure development, media, phone banks, and lawn signs. Your choice, of course, is dictated by your resources and the type of campaign you are running. For instance, you may not be able to afford direct mail even though you'd love to do it, or you may have decided you do not want to do lawn signs because they are unnecessary in the ballot measure election for which you're campaigning.

Once you have the list of campaign tasks, all you need to do is transfer them onto your campaign flow-chart in the proper sequence. A mock up of a campaign flow-chart is included in this chapter, as well as a blank flow-chart in the Appendix. Please feel free to copy it for your campaign use.

Building Your Campaign Flow-chart

A campaign flow-chart is an essential tool in any successful campaign. It is helpful for the campaign team because they can see the plan of the

"Simply reacting to the present demand or scrambling because of tensions is the opposite of thoughtful planning. Planning emphasizes conscious, disciplined choice."

Vaughn Keeler

whole campaign. Flow-charts keep the campaign organized. I have also found that the chart can have a calming effect on the candidate and staff because it clearly outlines exactly what needs to be done and when. I like to do my flow-charts in color.

To construct your flow-chart, you will need a long, unbroken wall, and you will need to gather the following items:

- *Five or more Post-it pads in assorted colors*
- *Butcher or freezer paper*
- *At least six different colored marking pens*
- *A yard stick*
- *Masking tape*
- *One or two key campaign people (no more) to help you think*

If possible, pull in someone who has worked on other campaigns to help you. An experienced campaigner will be an invaluable aide in building the flow-chart.

To begin your chart, unroll about ten feet of butcher paper and tape it up to a wall. On the far right bottom of the chart, place the date of the day after the election. On the far left, bottom, place the date of the beginning of your campaign. It may be the date that you start your flow-chart or the date when your first "formal" campaign activity (such as your announcement) is to take place. Draw a single line along the bottom between the two dates.

Divide the line into fairly equal monthly or weekly parts by drawing in all the dates between the day that your campaign begins and the day your campaign will end. Next, using a Post-it of a different color for each campaign function, begin brainstorming with your helpers and slapping up on the butcher paper the appropriately colored sticklet above the date that you want to do that particular campaign function. For example, if lawn signs are represented by green Post-its, put one that says "take down lawn signs" on the day after the election because you know that your crew will have to take down lawn signs on that day.

Work your way backwards from the end of the campaign, making decisions as you go. For instance, you know you will need to repair lawn signs the day after Halloween, so put that on a green Post-it above the 31st of October. Lawn signs go up usually one month before an election, so put that up next. You'll need a work party to get the signs stapled if you're using poly tag. This is a clerical function, so choose a different color. Write on the Post-it "staple lawn signs," and put it up somewhere in the week before the signs are to go up.

"First things first . . . And other things not at all."

Peter Drucker

Keep working your way back, thinking through each of the campaign activities you have on your list. Think in terms of the progression of an activity.

To continue the lawn-sign example, you will need stakes before you can start putting up signs. Decide on a date that doesn't clash with other lawn-sign activities such as stapling and label the Post-it as "get stakes made." Ask yourself, when will the signs be printed? Make up your mind and label the Post-it as "print lawn signs." Naturally, before they can get printed, you must have them designed and camera ready. You might want to allow two weeks for this. So, two weeks before the lawn signs are due to go to the printer, affix a Post-it that says, "design lawn signs." Continue in this fashion for each and every function. Some functions will flow into others. For instance, fund raising goes everywhere. The clerical team supports a number of activities, some of which may be happening at the same time. Use an arrow from the clerical line down to the appropriate activity line to show the connection. Should dates start to bunch up, move your activity dates around and keep track of them with your Post-its.

Spread Out the Activities

With this method, time periods with too much campaign activity become immediately apparent. For example, if you find by the concentration of multicolored Post-its that brochure development, two direct mail pieces, and a phone bank for an event are all happening at the same time, you may consider moving something to another time slot. For example, brochure development could move up and be done sooner, and the direct mail pieces may be handled this once by a mail-order house, or get prepared earlier or later. Your Post-its are mobile for a reason, and you want to take advantage of this during this campaign planning activity. Spread out the activities so you and the volunteers do not get overworked or burned out. If nothing can move, it will give you an opportunity to line up extra help to organize the work.

By placing colored stickers for every function in a campaign on the chart, you build a visual representation of the campaign. The process is simple: just take whatever it is that you want to do, give it a color, and work your way back from the date that you want to see that function completed to the point where that task must start in order to be completed on time. Some of the functions will end when others begin. For example, your brochure must be done in time to canvass. If canvassing will take you two months, working each day after work plus weekends, then your brochure must be developed

"A perfection of means and a confusion of aims seem to be our main problem."

Albert Einstein

and back from the printer by this time. Therefore, your Post-its for brochure development and printing will end on the flow-chart before your canvassing begins.

The Activities

Here is a partial list of activities that should be represented on your flow-chart:

- *Ads, print, radio, and TV*
- *Lawn signs, big and small*
- *Coffees, fund-raisers, special events*
- *Letters-to-the-editor*
- *Direct mail*
- *Brochure development*
- *Canvassing and precinct analysis*
- *Phone banks*

Once all your Post-its are up where you want them, you are ready to put together your permanent campaign flow-chart. Take another ten feet of butcher paper, your colored marking pens, and a yard stick. Lay the butcher paper on the floor in front of the Post-it flow-chart. If there is room, you can hang the new chart on the wall directly below the old one. Now all you have to do is write in and make permanent your campaign commitments on the dates listed. Follow your color scheme. For example, if lawn signs were in green Post-its, use a green marking pen for lawn signs on the flow-chart.

Above the various dates, write the activity that is on the Post-it for that date, then draw a line in the same color to the next date or activity, and so on until you have transferred everything from the Post-it covered chart. By using colored lines, at a glance you will be able to follow a particular activity across the whole campaign. Look at the accompanying example of a typical general election race. It's not as difficult as it sounds, and a flow-chart is definitely well worth the effort.

Example of Campaign Flow-chart
(see next page)

ﾛ

"Time is nature's way of keeping everything from happening at once."
     Woody Allen

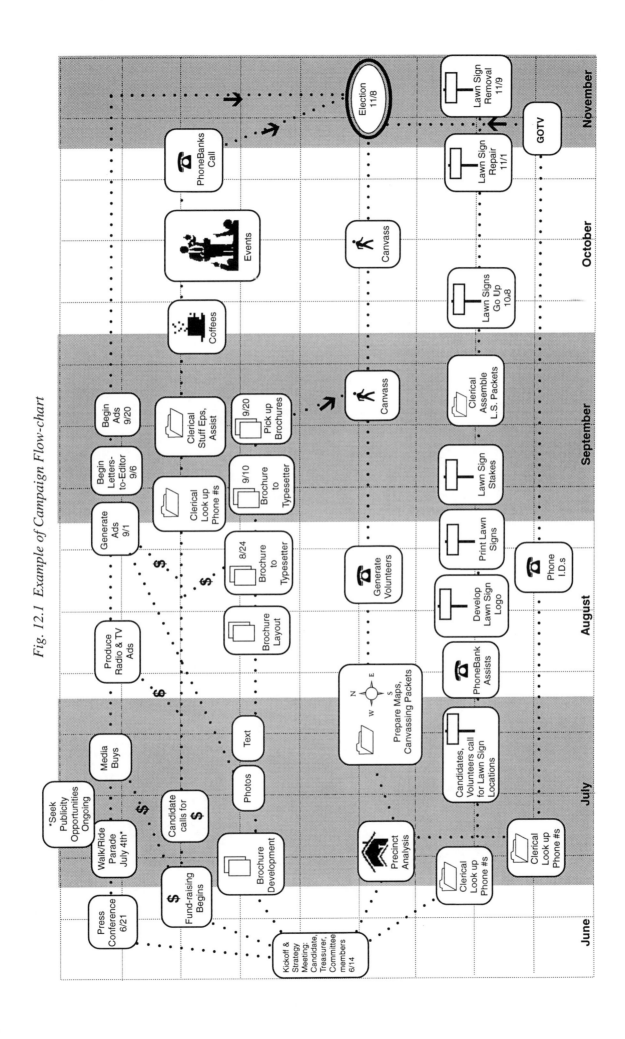

Fig. 12.1 Example of Campaign Flow-chart

Chapter 13

After the Ball

There are many things you must do to put your campaign to bed, win or lose. However, before taking down your lawn signs, bundling your stakes, paying your bills, finishing reports for the state, closing out bank accounts, and reassembling your house, you must first face election night.

On election night, if you are not in a well-known location with other candidates and their volunteer teams, you should let the press know where they can find you. I have held campaign parties in restaurants and at my home. I prefer my home. In the last days of the campaign, I let my volunteers know that I will be home and throwing a party in honor of a great campaign. I live in a small town, and so people call and stop by all night. It is difficult to stay home and watch returns alone if you have been involved in a campaign, especially a winning one. Most people drop by to share the excitement, even if it is just for a few minutes. My home is open.

If your campaign was one that covered an area larger than one city, you might need to go to a more central and public location. Again, tell all your volunteers where you will be and invite them. I try to spend election day or even the weekend before the election calling and personally thanking my volunteers. This is also a good time to remind them to join me on election night. Don't wait to thank them until after the election. If you lose, volunteers are anxious to talk and reflect and comfort, and you are anxious to sit alone on the floor of a dark closet.

There is no preparing for a loss, and I'm not even sure people *ever* get over it. It will change your life, just as winning will. But win or lose, you must be prepared to face the media and do it with class.

"Experience is not what happens to a person, it is what a person does with what happens."
Aldous Huxley

In one election on which I worked, I sat with the candidate as the first big returns came in. The shock that went through us as we realized we were losing is unexplainable. I remember cameras pointing at our faces. There is something predatory and morose about our society when it comes to watching a leader fall. We had expected a win and were not prepared for what was before us.

The next day our pictures were in the paper. I looked for shock, disbelief, upset, disappointment. None of it was in our faces. We just sat, stunned, looking at the huge TV in the restaurant. In the story that followed, the candidate thanked his volunteers, his campaign team, his supporters. He thanked everyone for a chance to serve. The end.

Win or lose, that is the speech. You must be graceful and appreciative. If you win, you must be humble and immediately begin mending fences that might have been broken during the process. Win or lose, you thank your family, volunteers, supporters, and the community for support. If you lose, there is one more call you must make, and that is to your opponent. Congratulate that person and say that you are on board to help make his or her time in office as successful as possible.

In my second bid for mayor, we won handily, by nearly two to one. On election night my house was full of friends and volunteers. Well wishers phoned. Everyone brought something to eat and drink. Then a reporter called. He said that one of my opponents was convinced that he had lost because of a damaging letter-to-the-editor that accused him of criminal wrongdoing 20 years ago. The reporter said my opponent had suggested I was responsible for the letter.

Although I had nothing to do with this letter and the accusation was without merit, it made me feel like the campaign wasn't over.

Have you ever watched a game where the coach for the losing team says basically it's no wonder we lost: we made mistakes or didn't play our best? While it may make that person feel better, it makes the winning team feel slighted.

Be graceful. If you lost, say you put together a great effort but that your opponent put together a better one. Give your opponent a little of the limelight if you won and a lot of the limelight if you lost. Don't blame your loss on insufficient campaign effort. That translates to: my volunteers are responsible for this loss. The most common feeling of volunteers of a losing campaign is, "What a waste of time that was." Say you had a great campaign team who put

"The two happiest days of my life were the day we moved into the White House and the day we moved out."

    Betty Ford

in countless hours and that the whole thing was a ball, challenging, instructive, and fun from beginning to end. Take heart in the fact that you have come to know yourself and the democratic process better.

Should you ever run for office again, you will be glad you acted magnanimously.

Afterword

You are now prepared to begin on that time-honored path of a political campaign. Campaigns are enormously fun and exhilarating. If you do everything right, you are almost assured a win. Just a few reminders before you begin:

1. Know the law.

2. Stay on your campaign theme or message, and you will be in control.

3. Deliver that message to your targeted voters: "aim at the souls that can be saved."

4. Redirect negative campaigning at your opponents and use it as an opportunity to restate your message.

5. Work hard and others will work hard for you.

6. Be humble and listen more than you speak.

7. Know who you are before others find out.

Win or lose, you will emerge from the process a different person, a leader within your community.

"The great use of life is to spend it for something that outlasts it."
William James

About the Author

Cathy Golden is currently serving in her second term as Mayor of Ashland, Oregon. First elected in 1988, she was the youngest mayor as well as the first woman mayor in the history of the city. She has managed local campaigns for 10 years with a success rate of 82 percent. Combining the power of elected office with campaigning expertise, Cathy has successfully managed campaigns to pass innovative taxing measures for funding public education, recreation, parks, and open-space programs.

Outspent in every election, sometimes as much as five to one, Cathy has developed and perfected techniques to combat big money and engineer seemingly impossible wins. She has been a frequent guest speaker and instructor for political science classes and campaign schools.

Cathy is available for teaching at campaign schools and for telephone and on-site consultations. Please contact Oak Street Press for details.

Appendix:
Forms

For
Photocopying

FORM 1
ELECTION DATA FORM

Candidate _____   **County** _____

Election Date _____   **Page** ___ **of** ___ **Pages**

Pre-cinct	Reg. Voters	Reg. Demos.	Dem. T/O	Reg. Repubs.	Rep. T/O							Dem. U/V	Rep. U/V

FORM 2

PRECINCT TARGETING WORKSHEET

H/S Support	H/T Turnout
M/S	M/T
L/S	L/T

FORM 3

PRECINCT PRIORITIES WORKSHEET

(1) H/S + L/T = High Priority	(6) M/S + H/T = Medium Priority
(2) H/S + M/T = High Priority	(7) L/S + L/T = Low Priority
(3) M/S + L/T = High Priority	(8) L/S + M/T = Low Priority
(4) M/S + M/T = Medium Priority	(9) L/S + H/T = Low Priority
(5) H/S + H/T = Medium Priority	

FORM 4

TARGETING PRIORITIES & STRATEGY WORKSHEET

Prio-rity	Pre-cinct	Reg. Voters	Party Density	Support	T/O	U/V	Precinct Location	Campaign Strategy

FORM 5

BALLOT MEASURE FORM

Precinct	Reg. Voters	Turnout	Count Yes	Count No	Turnout %	% Yes	% No	UV

FORM 6

SWING VOTERS FORM

Priority	Precinct	Reg. Voters	Reg. Demos.	Party Density % Demo.	Reg. Repubs.	Party Density % Repub.	Support Yes	Support No

FORM 7

VOLUNTEER SIGN-UP SHEET

I would like to volunteer for the following (please check all that apply):

Name (please print)	Home Phone	Canvass Neighborhoods	Phone Banks	Lawn Sign Location	Donation

FORM 8

FLOW-CHART GRID

Index

To Order Additional Copies

Please send the following: **Qty.**   **Cost**

        The Campaign Manager   @ $24.95   ____   ____

        plus shipping priority mail $5.00   ____   ____

                                           Total   ____

☎ Call toll free: **1 (800) 299-1023 or**

      Fax Orders: **1 (541) 482-1427 or**

✉ Mail this form to: **Oak Street Press**
                                886 Oak St.
                                Ashland, OR 97520-1265
                                USA

Visit our web page at: **http://www.cdsnet.net/Business/OakPress/**

Or email us at: **oakpress@cdsnet.net**

Name _____

Address _____

Phone _____ Fax _____

Payment ____ Visa ____ Master Card ____ Discover Card ____ Check (Payable to Oak Street Press)

Name as it appears on Card _____ Number _____

Exp. Date _____ Cardholder's Signature _____

ISBN 0-9650761-0-5

Quantity Discounts Available

Call toll free and order now